BLUENOSES, BEARS AND BANDITS

Sea Service to Commandos

An account of some events in the service life of the author
William J Kitchingham

Series Editor
Colonel Brian Carter OBE RM

ROYAL MARINES HISTORICAL SOCIETY
SPECIAL PUBLICATION NO 43

Bluenoses, Bears And Bandits

978-1-908123-12-1

First published 2015 by the
ROYAL MARINES HISTORICAL SOCIETY
Royal Marines Museum
Eastney
Southsea
Hants PO4 9PX
United Kingdom

Cover, design and layout
Tim Mitchell
www.tim-mitchell.co.uk

Printed and bound in Great Britain by
CPI Antony Rowe Ltd, Chippenham and Eastbourne

Contents

Acknowledgements

In writing this book I have called upon my recollection of events as I remembered them and, in order to be accurate with the units and dates, I have referred to the official entries in my Service Documents. My old photographs were a great help in refreshing my memory.

I am thankful for the items published by the General Information Office in The Daily Yorker, and The Sunday Yorker, the ship's newsheets of *HMS Duke of York*.

I am grateful to The Keeper of Public Records, Kew, and The Director, Royal Marines Museum, Eastney, for their assistance.

My thanks go to Anne for her encouragement in this project.

Preface

One day not so long ago, Margaret, my third daughter said to me that she had been hearing a great deal about peoples' experiences during World War Two, and the problems of living in Great Britain in those wartime days, but she knew very little of my service career and thought it would be a good idea if I were to write an account of it so that she could answer her children's questions about their grandfather.

When I was tracing our family tree some years ago, I thought that, apart from the usual facts of births, marriages and deaths, it would have been very interesting to know more of our ancestors, so Margaret's suggestion hit a chord in me. I said that I agreed with her and that it would be a good project for me now that I am retired.

Therefore, in memory of my wife, Patricia, and for the interest of our daughters Beverley, Elizabeth, Margaret and Yvonne, and their families this is an account of some of my personal experiences and of the many interesting places to where my thirty-seven years' service in the Royal Marines had taken me.

I chose the title because the words represent specific periods of my service career. 'Bluenoses' comes from the Bluenose Certificate which personnel who crossed the Arctic Circle in one of HM Ships received. I crossed the Arctic Circle many times during 1944 while serving onboard *HMS Jamaica*.

'Bears' comes from the traditional Crossing the Line ceremony, the line being the Equator. King Neptune rises from the deep and enquires if there is anyone onboard who has not previously crossed the Line. The Bears are part of his retinue and play a major part in this time-honoured seafarers' ceremony of initiating the novices. During 1945 and 1946 I served onboard *HMS Duke of York* in the Pacific area crossing the Line a number of times.

'Bandits', well, this was the term used by the Commandos when referring to terrorists in Malaya and other troubled regions of the World.

Chapter 1
Dundonald

There is one way to start a narrative such as this and that is at the beginning. We all have beginnings and ancestors. Many people have traced their family tree, their roots, and I am no different. My family name goes back to the early 1700s in the church records of the two neighbouring English villages of Hartlip and Rainham in the County of Kent. However, Kitchingham shows up in the records of East Sussex, and in the 1200s it was spelt, Ketchyngham.

I was born 'A Man of Kent' on the 24 April 1924 in Rainham, Kent. At that time Rainham was a small village between the towns of Gillingham and Sittingbourne on the Roman road, Watling Street, now known as the A2. My parents, with me as an infant in arms, moved to South Wales for a few months before moving to Middlesbrough where my sister, Mavis, was born. My father's work then required him to go to Belfast, Northern Ireland, so we moved there as a family in 1927. After staying in lodgings in Belfast close to the river Laggan for a few months, our parents rented a house in the quiet village of Dundonald, in the countryside of County Down, about five miles east of Belfast, on the main road to Newtownards. I went to school at Dundonald, except for a few months at Solomon Road School in Rainham, Kent. I was recovering from a mastoid operation at the time, and was living with my paternal grandmother.

As a family we made a number of summer holiday journeys, by sea and train between Dundonald and Kent, which were great adventures to us young children. Brother Edward was born in Kent on one of these visits when we were visiting our mother's parents. And brother Robin was born a few years later in Dundonald.

My sister, two brothers and I were involved in the village life of young children, and enjoyed being members of the local youth organisations. I was a member of the local Church of Ireland church choir, and took my turn to work the air pump for the church organ, and ring the church bell.

We had plenty of green fields with streams running through them, and woods in which to play. I once fell into a stream and got my cloths soaking wet, and was worried about what awaited me at home, but all was well after a telling off. Our bicycles gave us the freedom to roam the quiet lanes and peaceful countryside. So it was that we had a happy childhood at Dundonald. The peace of Dundonald, indeed the peace of the whole 'Ards Circuit', was shattered once a year in the summer time by the Ulster Tourist Trophy Motor Car Race Meeting. The 'Ards Circuit', as it was known, was about thirteen miles around each lap. The course was in County Down, in the form of a triangle, Dundonald to Newtownards to Comber and back to Dundonald, on public roads which were closed for the meeting. After a very tragic accident in Newtownards, where a number of spectators were killed when a racing car went out of control, the meeting was no longer held. I use to think it amazing that thousands of people would travel out of Belfast, from very early in the morning, by tram as far as the Dundonald Golf Club tram terminus, and then walk two or three miles or more, past our house, to get to vantage points to view the race.

When I left school I obtained a job in Short and Harland's aircraft factory in Belfast as a works apprentice, and attended the Belfast Technical College for classes on sheet metal working. For some months I worked in the fuel tank section for Handley Page Hampton bombers, testing the fuel tanks for leaks. Then I was moved to the main frame section for the Bristol Bombay bombers. There were also some Short Sunderland flying boats in the factory.

I remember as a lad months before war broke out, on two occasions, when I was cycling past the perimeter fencing of Newtownards Airfield, seeing a German three-engined Junkers 52 aircraft parked near the control block. The Swastika on the tailplane stood out in marked contrast on the silver painted background.

I was aged fifteen years and five months when I was in our garden and heard the voice of the Prime Minister, Mr N Chamberlain on the wireless, drifting through the open kitchen window saying, "and this country is now at war with Germany." It was sometime after 11.00 a.m. on the morning of the 3 September 1939. I must say I did not grasp the gravity of his declaration, but I was soon to find out.

The civil air raid precautions were put into operation. Blackout curtains were fixed to windows at dusk each evening to ensure that   no lights could be seen shining out in the dark. There were no street lights, and vehicles had to have special hoods fitted to their headlights to keep the beam shining down.

I became a member of the village Local Defence Volunteer Unit (LDV). Then we had the Air Raid Precautions (ARP), which later became the Civil Defence Corps. The local St John's Ambulance Association was calling for volunteers, so I enrolled for their classes and qualified as a First-Aider. I also qualified for the Home Nursing Certificate and then became an ambulance attendant.

One evening we heard the air raid warning sirens warbling the 'Alert' - the 'All Clear' was a long continuous note – and we put into practice what we had trained to do in such an event. It was 1940 and the German Air Force had started bombing many cities in the United Kingdom.

My place of duty was at the First-Aid Post in the village primary school, less than five minutes run from home. This was a new experience for us, but one to be repeated. The faint drone of aircraft engines drew closer from what seemed a large force of German bombers passing close to the village and heading for Belfast. Suddenly we heard our first stick of bombs exploding nearby, one after the other, the blasts fairly rattled the doors and windows of the First-Aid Post.

One night during a heavy bombing raid on Belfast our village ambulance team was called upon, with other units, to help with the casualties in the city. So our ambulance driver and I were dispatched to a control point in Belfast to receive our instructions.

What a mess lay before us. The Belfast Ropes Works was on fire, there were bomb craters in the streets and tram lines bent up in the air by the force of the exploding bombs. Fires caused by hundreds of small incendiary bombs were burning in many side streets, bricks and rubble were strewn over the roadways. Dust from collapsed buildings, smoke, and the smell of charred wood hung in the air.

Delayed action bombs were exploding somewhere in the city. A few planes were droning in the distance and anti-aircraft shells were bursting in the night sky. There was still the danger of being hit on the head by shrapnel falling from our defensive anti-aircraft shells - it was wise to wear your steel helmet during a raid.

We had been directed to the quayside where some ships were tied up. The local air raid wardens guided us to where the casualties were sheltering, and we made a couple of trips to a casualty clearing station with injured persons. Sadly, we also had to take a number of dead to a temporary mortuary. By now it was nearing dawn, but fires still lit up the wrecked city. The ruins of shattered homes and shops littered the streets and made progress with the ambulance slow at times as we made our way back to Dundonald. I was aged sixteen years.

Chapter 2
Stonehouse Barracks Plymouth

The war had been going on for two years now. I was still employed at the Short and Harland aircraft factory in Belfast, and for a spell I worked on the night shift. Air raids were still occurring, but not so heavy now.

When I was seventeen years and six months of age, I enlisted in the Royal Marines. I was one of a small group of volunteers who were routed from Belfast to the Royal Navy and Royal Marines Recruiting Office at Liverpool, where I was attested on the 7 October 1941. Later that day three of us for the Royal Marines were put on a train for Plymouth in Devon. We were met on arrival at Plymouth North Road railway station and taken to Stonehouse Barracks, which was the home base of the Plymouth Division, Royal Marines.

There were two other Divisions, one at Eastney Barracks, Southsea, Portsmouth, and the other at Chatham Barracks, Kent. I had no choice in choosing a Division but, as it turned out, the Plymouth Division was going to suit me just fine.

Stonehouse Barracks was built in the 1780s, and occupied a few years later, the accommodation blocks forming a rectangle around the parade ground. The clothing store, tailor's shop, armoury, cook-house, bath house, dhobying rooms and other facilities were located behind the main block, and linked by a drill shed which looked like a large bus garage. During inclement weather we carried out our parade work in the drill shed.

As soon as we were in the barracks we met up with a number of other young men, who had been arriving in small groups throughout the day, from all over the United Kingdom. I could not understand the speech of two lads from Musselburgh in Scotland, and it was nearly as difficult to follow the conversation of those from Bristol.

Forty-six of us were formed into a group to be known as the 404 Squad, a long service squad, and our training would last ten months. We were placed in the charge of a sergeant instructor who was assisted by a lance corporal. A number of other squads were in barracks at various stages in their training. Some were HO Squads - Hostilities Only - with a shorter training period.

Dressed in khaki battledress, and unaccustomed to marching about as a group of men, we commenced our training and soon progressed from an awkward looking bunch into a co-ordinated squad. I am sure we tried the patience of our sergeant many a time. Our syllabus included periods of physical training in the gymnasium where our physical measurements were recorded at intervals to see how we were filling-out, none of us was in any way fat on enlistment. Regular medical and dental checks were made on us, and there was the standard swimming test to pass. Corps history lectures were also a feature in our training.

The areas of Plymouth and Devonport had suffered greatly from the German bombers, however, Stonehouse Barracks had suffered only minor damage. It was a shame to see the once fine houses, in the residential areas around the barracks, so badly damaged. Under the parade ground were air raid shelters where we would have to go when the 'Alert' sounded, and we spent a few anxious nights in them during the early weeks of our training. Later we were formed into working parties for duties in the barracks, such as lookouts, fire-fighting, rescue and first-aid parties. Some of us young recruits had already experienced bombing by the German Air Force, so we had a practiced ear for the drone of aircraft engines in detecting if the planes were coming overhead, or were likely to pass clear of us.

The 404 Squad on parade, Stonehouse Barracks, Plymouth November 1941.

After a couple of months in barracks under basic training we were moved to Blarrick Camp for further training in small arms and fieldcraft. Being an open air lad at heart I quite enjoyed it, and looked forward to the rifle shooting on the nearby Tregantel ranges, which were on the red earth cliffs overlooking the English Channel. Blarrick Camp at this time was a tented affair and was later developed into a Nissen hut camp. It was near the small Cornish village of St Anthony, a few miles inland from Torpoint. St Anthony had the nearest pub to the camp, the Ring O' Bells, and the village hall where dances were held. The local girls always turned out for the dances, they looked forward to them just as much as we did. Our sergeant instructor was a native of St Anthony and he was very concerned that we should behave ourselves and not let him down in the eyes of the locals. I think we were quite well behaved, for young lads.

Towards the end of our training, I was one of six recruits of our squad who were selected to become Section Commanders. Apparently we had shown promise, and the right attitude during our training. We had to wear a red diamond patch at the top of the left sleeve of our uniforms to indicate our selection. Being a Section Commander would give us six months seniority for promotion. We had been given lectures on the promotion procedures, and the specialists courses available to us after we had completed six months service in a unit after passing for duty.

When the squad, in its turn, became the senior long service squad in barracks and was within a month of passing for duty, we had the honour of being designated the 'King's Squad'. To denote that we were the 'King's Squad' we had to wear the chin strap of our caps down around our chins. It was now nearing our passing out parade, and time for the selection of 'King's Badgeman' to be made for the recruit who had set the highest standard during training. The Adjutant said that the six section commanders had all set equally high standards and that it would be unfair to single out one of us. So there was to be no 'King's Badgeman' for the 404 Squad. This was a great disappointment to the four ex-buglers who had transferred from Bugler to Marine and who were in our Squad for training. They had an advantage over us raw recruits of several years' service each, and knew the ways of the Corps. They had been looking forward to one of them being awarded the King's Badge. I felt very pleased with myself that I had been considered amongst the top best recruits.

There were a number of highlights during our training, one being the visit, in the summer of 1942, of HM King George VI to Stonehouse Barracks. Such a visit required a Royal Guard of Honour of one hundred men, which was made up of the 404 Squad and Marines from other squads in barracks. After we presented arms with the Royal Salute the King inspected the Guard, walking up and down the ranks, stopping and saying a few words to individuals. I was thrilled when he spoke to me and asked how long I had been in the Corps.

The 404 Squad passed for duty on the 1 August 1942. It was a very pleasant day, and I must say we did present ourselves as a fine, dependable and well trained squad. Some good friendships had been made during our time together, and now we wondered what lay ahead.

Upon returning from leave we checked the drafting noticeboard to see where we were to be posted. Most of my squad mates were to be posted overseas but I was to remain in barracks as a lance corporal and be a rear rank instructor. Our former sergeant instructor was to be in charge of the next intake of recruits and I was to be his assistant. I was quite excited at the prospect. We would be training a hostilities only squad, the HO212 Squad.

A few days after I started wearing my lance corporal stripe, I was asked to go to the Sergeants' Mess and help two sergeants, who were in a hurry, with their uniforms and fighting equipment, which I did, and off they went in transport which was waiting for them at the mess front door. I thought they were called away for a training exercise but, it turned out that they were part of the British contingent in the ill-fated Dieppe Raid on the 18-19 August 1942, in which the main assaulting Canadian troops suffered a severe number of casualties. Apparently the German coastal defence troops in the Dieppe area had not been surprised by the attack. When the two sergeants returned to barracks they were fairly tired and very dirty. One of them had what is known as flash blindness and could not see very well so, after he got cleaned up and put on fresh clothing, he went to the sick bay for treatment. The other sergeant had a bullet hole through his water bottle. It was unnervingly obvious that he had had a lucky escape from a bullet so close to his body. I took their equipment and uniforms away for cleaning.

The nominal roll of the forty-four members of the 404 King's Squad which passed for duty at Stonehouse Barracks, Plymouth on the 1 August 1942:

ATKINSON E	KIDD R
BADMAN N R	KITCHINGHAM W J
BEGGS S D	KNOX R J
BOSWELL J	LANGLEY P W T
BRICKNELL T G	LISTER R
BUTCHER P	MELLOR K R
CLARK W	MITCHELL R J
CLEGG J	O'NEILL C
CUNNINGHAM W C	PEPOLE R J
DAVIES S	PERRY L
DIDCOTT S G	POPE K
DODD D	ROSS A
FRANCIS K	ROYLE F
GODSELL J A GRAYSON L	STEWART A
HATFIELD R L	STUBBS C E
HATHERALL J W E	TAYLOR D P
HAWES J A	WALLACE L
HINTON J	WEAGER W
HOLMES R	WOOSTER J
HOLT J	WYNNE K A
HONEYSETT K	YOUNG R Y M
JAMES J	

As I was now a lance corporal it meant that I would be in charge of a barrack room of new intake recruits, so I moved into a corner bed. Corner beds in recruit company rooms were usually the perks of the 'old soldier'. I now had more freedom of movement and privileges as well as the extra duties. There were a number of corporals and lance corporals in the recruit company and all of us set an example for the new recruits to follow.

Stonehouse Barracks had that solid feel about it, good order and discipline. Bugle calls controlled the daily routine from 'Reveille' to 'Lights-out'. The young buglers took a great pride in the clarity of their bugle calls. 'Sunset' and 'Last Post' gave them the opportunity to show their skill, I must say that it was quite stirring to hear the bugle calls echoing across the parade ground and around the barrack blocks.

Plymouth Division, Royal Marines.

SPECIAL ORDER OF THE DAY.

By General Sir W. W. Godfrey, K.C.B., C.M.G.,
Hon. Colonel Commandant, Plymouth Division, R.M.

As Honorary Colonel Commandant, it has given me great pleasure to visit my Division—I have been greatly impressed by the bearing and smartness displayed by all ranks, proving that the high sense of discipline in the Division is being well maintained.

The standard attained by the 404th King's Squad was very good. I was especially pleased to witness their passing for duty.

Difficult times may be ahead of us. What I have seen today gives me renewed confidence regarding the ultimate issue of the conflict.

I wish all ranks the best of good fortune.

W. W. GODFREY,
General.

1st August, 1942.

Our beds were quite comfortable, and something of a surprise to many. The Barrack Master arranged for a regular supply of fresh straw for us to change the contents of our palliasses. Normal mattresses had not yet been introduced into the barrack rooms. One had to be careful to stuff just the right amount of straw into the palliasse; too much and your bed was too high, too little and your hips would rest on the metal slats of the bed frame. Sometimes, as we lay in our beds at night, we would hear the unmistakeable sound of the four-engined RAF Short Sunderland flying boats of Coastal Command taking off from the waters of Plymouth Sound, and head out on their long range anti U-boat patrols over the seas of the Western Approaches. When I worked in the aircraft factory at Belfast I had a few opportunities to have a good look around the Sunderlands, and could picture in my mind's eye the inside of the flying boats as they took-off on their missions.

From where Stonehouse Barracks was situated in Durnford Street, it was quite easy to go for nice walks, when time and duty allowed. Sometimes to the Cremyl Ferry hard or out around Eastern Kings and Devil's Point to watch ships passing up and down the Hamoaze, in and out of the Royal Navy's base at Devonport on the river Tamar. It was also most pleasant on a calm moonlit night to sit quietly by the sea wall at Devil's Point and listen to the sea lapping gently against the rocks, but it was another story when a southwest gale was blowing in from the English Channel.

Another walk was to Plymouth Hoe, where Drake's statue stood, to sit on the high grassy slopes of the Hoe and gaze out to sea, past Drake's Island and the breakwater of Plymouth Sound, towards the Eddystone Lighthouse many miles distant. On a good day the Eddystone could be seen standing beside the stump of a previous lighthouse which had been dismantled, re-erected and preserved on Plymouth Hoe. It was not far then to walk on to the Barbican and the Mayflower Steps from where the Pilgrim Fathers sailed to the new world in the *Mayflower* in the year 1620, and there founded the new settlement of Plymouth.

We had in Stonehouse one of the most famous military bands in the United Kingdom at that time, The Band of the Royal Marines, Plymouth Division, under the direction of Major Rickets, who composed music under the name of Kenneth Alford. Often during the day we would hear the band in their practice room being put through their paces, and it was great to hear them on parade. The band had a distinctive sound of its own, we could easily recognise it on the radio. During the war years the band gave many concerts on the BBC radio, broadcast from the Globe Theatre right in the heart of the barracks.

One morning towards the end of October 1943, I think it was the 22nd, one of our Marine friends came into the barrack room in a bit of a temper, bemoaning the fact that he had just been given a 'pier head jump', that is, an immediate drafting to a ship without pre-embarkation leave. He was required to join the Royal Navy's anti-aircraft cruiser, *HMS Charybdis*, which was in Devonport, by mid-afternoon.

He packed his kit bags, and those of us who were in the room at the time wished him good luck and expressed the hope of seeing him again sometime. We shook hands, and he got into a vehicle waiting for him at the main gate to take him the mile or so to Devonport Dockyard to join his ship.

But, at breakfast next morning we were stunned at the 'buzz' that had just gone round the barracks. *HMS Charybdis*, which had gone out on a patrol with a number of destroyers last evening, had been sunk by enemy action during the night, out in the English Channel, not long after leaving Plymouth Sound. Many of the ship's company were lost, including forty two Royal Marines. *HMS Charybdis* was a Plymouth ship, that is, the Royal Marine Detachment was from Stonehouse Barracks, and the Naval Ratings were from the Royal Naval Barracks, Devonport.

Later in the day our room-mate was back in barracks. He had been one of the small number of survivors who had been rescued by one of the destroyers and brought back to Devonport. He was back, twenty-four hours after leaving, and mad as hell at losing his kit. Apparently he had a number of personal items in his kitbags, and was upset at their loss. In fact we all had our own personal items, photographs and keepsakes which we treasured, so we sympathized in his misfortune.

He was a good Marine and well-liked by those who knew him. We knew he was shocked by his experience. Nevertheless, some bright spark taunted him with, "Now you can get survivors leave!"

Chapter 3
Quebec

Towards the end of July 1943, I was one of a small group of Royal Marines from Stonehouse Barracks who had been selected to make up a special detachment to be known as 'Party Med'. We were given a general briefing and warned not to discuss it with anyone. The duties of the Royal Marine Detachment were to provide orderlies for the Prime Minister and Chiefs of Staff, and during moves to handle and guard the secret documents, and assist with the personal luggage of the Special Party. Sentries and armed guards were to be provided as necessary.

We travelled by rail from Plymouth to London and upon our arrival we split up into small working parties to collect sensitive stores from Government offices, and VIP baggage from certain addresses in London. I was required to go to Chartwell in a chauffeur driven armoured, black ministerial car to collect baggage marked Colonel Warden, the name under which Mr Churchill was travelling. It was quite late in the evening and dark when we headed back to London. As soon as the special train was loaded with its passengers and baggage, and a final check made that all was well, it left London for the overnight journey to Scotland with Royal Marines on guard.

We embarked in the giant Cunard liner *Queen Mary*, 81,000 tons, and sailed from the Clyde p.m. on the 5 August 1943. The *Queen Mary* soon picked up her normal speed, and anti U-boat zigzag course, for the four day crossing of the North Atlantic to Halifax, Canada.

Once at sea we were given a further briefing and informed of our tasks. I was assigned, with three other lance corporals, to the Prime Minister's office. During the sea passage we soon got to know the Prime Minister's staff. There was Mr John Martin the Principal Private Secretary, Mr Leslie Rowan a Private Secretary, Mr Patrick Kinna the PM's clerk, and other Private and Personal Secretaries. There was also Commander C R Thompson RN ADC, Inspector W H Thompson (ex Special Branch Scotland Yard), the PM's shadow/bodyguard, and Mr Frank Sawyers the PM's butler. Another essential person to know of was Captain R P Pim RNVR who was in charge of the PM's Map Room.

Very important staff meetings took place as we crossed the Atlantic. On one occasion, I was on duty outside the PM's cabin where he was having a meeting with the Chiefs of Staff and other senior officers, when a very senior naval officer opened the cabin door and said to me, "Put a few inches of cold water in the bath and let me know when it is ready", which I did. A number of curious looking models were then taken into the bathroom and placed on the surface of the water. The PM and his staff then continued their meeting in an over-crowded bathroom. I was later to learn that,

in that bathroom, a discussion on the Mulberry project took place - this was the creation of artificial harbours which were to be located close to the Normandy beaches to enable supply ships to unload essential war materials for the Allied armies.

The *Queen Mary* arrived at Halifax p.m. on the 9 August 1943. The Conference delegation soon disembarked and, with their baggage, boarded a special train provided by the Canadian National Railways.

Whilst the special stores were being transferred from ship to train the area was placed under armed guard. I was armed with a naval sub-machine gun - a Lanchester, loaded with a 50 round magazine of 9mm ammunition - and posted out on the railway sidings. A number of red-coated Mounties were also in the area.

There was a moment when, out of the corner of my eye, I noticed Mr Churchill, who was not many yards away walking up and down for exercise before getting on the train, gazing thoughtfully past me into the distance.

Later in the afternoon the train started out on its 500 mile journey through the Canadian Provinces of Nova Scotia, New Brunswick and into Quebec where we arrived p.m. on the 10 August. The evening meal for us young servicemen who were used to austerity, was a delight, and we spent a very comfortable night in sleeping berths prepared by the coach attendants. There were official photographers onboard the train and a group of us were photographed in a coach, all looking very pleased with ourselves.

At Quebec, the Prime Minister stayed at the Citadel, to be joined later by the American President, Mr Roosevelt. The Conference delegations of both sides were accommodated in a Canadian Pacific Hotel, the picturesque Chateau Frontenac. I remember their advertising slogan, 'Snow's Right, Sun's Bright, Ski in Friendly old Quebec.' We orderlies and some of the Royal Marine sentries were housed in outbuildings within the battlements of the Citadel. It was here that we came into full contact with the Royal Canadian Mounted Police. They were in charge of the security arrangements for the Conference. Red Coats were on duty within the Citadel and the Hotel.

One day I was watching a small, four legged animal with a bushy tail scurrying across the lawns at the Citadel when one of the Mounties came out of a doorway and very quickly said, "Keep away from that! It's a skunk!"

On the 13th, I was paired up with one of the other lance corporals for a trip away from the main body. We were to take some dispatches to the Prime Minister who had gone to visit Mr Roosevelt, the President of the United States of America, at his home at Hyde Park, near Poughkeepsie, New York State. We flew the 400 miles in a twin-engined airplane made available by the Governor General of Canada, from Quebec to an American airfield near Hyde Park. On arrival, we were met by United States officials and taken by car to the President's home, where we handed the pouch to the PM's Principal Private Secretary. Whilst we were in the President's home, I noticed gently sloping ramps which had been fitted at the changes of levels in the corridor for the President's wheelchair. We had a pleasant surprise when Mrs Roosevelt came upon us, and enquired how we were after the flight. We replied that we were fine, and she said that if there was anything we wanted just please ask. The PM's Principal Private Secretary informed us that we would have to stay the night and take a pouch back to Quebec next morning. So an American escort drove us to the nearby town of Poughkeepsie where reservations had been made for us at the Nelson House Hotel.

After a meal we took a walk along Main Street to stretch our legs. It was now dark and we remarked on the street lights and the window displays. The evening was quite warm so we went into a drug store and had a Coke each before returning to the hotel.

Our return journey was not going to be as straightforward as the flight from Quebec. We were picked up after breakfast by car from the Nelson House Hotel and taken to Hyde Park where we collected the bag from the PM's Principal Private Secretary. US officials then escorted us back to the airfield and we boarded the same plane that brought us.

During the take-off run along the runway there was an engine failure in one of the plane's engines which caused immediate concern to all in the plane. However, the pilot did a magnificent job in aborting the take off at the end of the runway. As the aircraft came to rest there was a rapid evacuation of the plane, fire being a real possibility. A car rushed out to meet us and took us all back to the airfield control offices. After some discussion, the Americans arranged for one of their airplanes, I think it was a Dakota, to fly us back to Canada. On nearing Quebec, the pilot received a radio report that there was fog at Quebec and that we were to divert to Montreal.

Canadian officials met us when we landed, and whilst driving us into the city explained that reservations had been made for us on the overnight train from Montreal to Quebec. As the train was not due to leave for a few hours yet it was suggested that, if we were feeling hungry, we could have a meal in a restaurant near the station. The Canadian officials, who were dressed in civilian clothing said that we need not worry about anything, they would be close-by while we ate our meal, and they would see us onto the train in good time. We were dressed in our normal navy blue uniforms and peak hats. My colleague, Ken, said, "OK then." And when we got into the city he looked around and, indicating a restaurant, said, "Let's go in there and see what they've got." We went in and a waitress took our orders. I asked for crayfish as I had never tasted one before. Whilst waiting for our food we went into the toilet to freshen ourselves up after the flight. As we ate our food we discussed the events of the past few hours. There were few customers in the place, nevertheless, we kept the pouch, which had to be guarded at all times, out of view as best we could.

We finished our meal, paid the bill and left the restaurant. I had been hungry and enjoyed the crayfish.

We walked along the pavement, which was quite wide, towards the Montreal railway station, a few hundred yards away. We looked at shop window displays as we passed making remarks such as, "You can't get that back home", or "Look at that". Then, in the reflection of a shop window I saw some men closing in on us from behind. Their manner of approach alerted me and I said to my colleague, who at this time was on my right and carrying the pouch in his left hand, "Look out Ken, something's happening!" He replied, "Yes! I've seen them." I slipped my right hand down and also took hold of the handle of the pouch. Three men closed in on us and one tried to snatch the pouch away. I exclaimed, "What do you think you're doing? Leave our music case alone, we're bandsmen." At that moment the three strangers and ourselves were surrounded by a group of our plain clothed Canadian friends, who had been keeping an eye on us. The Officer in Charge told us everything was under control and that we should carry on to the railway station.

As I looked back, I saw the three men being bundled into some waiting cars. We entered the station, boarded the train for Quebec and found our sleeping berths. We could not undress and turn-in, we had to take it in turns to snatch some sleep. One of us simply had to be awake and guard the pouch.

On our arrival at Quebec early next morning a car was waiting and took us back to the Citadel where we handed the pouch to the duty private secretary in the PM's office. Back in our quarters we were greeted by the off duty RM Guards with, "What happened to you two, get lost, eh?" Our Colour Sergeant in charge ordered us to get cleaned up, and have some breakfast. There would be another briefing about the Conference duties later in the afternoon.

The 26 August 1943 saw me taking dispatches from the PM's base office at the Citadel to Snow Lake - Lac des Neiges - up in the mountains of Laurentian Park, about sixty five miles from Quebec. The Prime Minister was resting at a fishing camp following the end of the Quebec Conference. A Canadian Army driver with a staff car drove me into the Park area. As we went deeper into the forest I kept a lookout for wild life amongst the trees and tall scrub, but none was to be seen. Eventually we came to a landing stage on the edge of a lake. It was nearing dusk as a small motorboat took me the rest of the journey along the lake to the camp, which was a small group of traditional Canadian log cabins, where I handed the pouch to the PM's Secretary. The weather now was a little chilly, however, I had a good meal, and a comfortable night's sleep in a bunk bed in one of the log cabins.

Next morning, the 27th, Inspector W H Thompson, the PM's shadow, said to me that he was in need of a second person to go out on the lake with him with the VIP fishing party, so I found myself paddling a Canadian canoe. I knew nothing about the technique required to paddle a Canadian canoe. Although I had seen films of Red Indians in their canoes I never thought the time would come when I would be in one. The other important personalities were already out on the tree lined lake in small craft, casting their fishing lines. All was peaceful and quiet.

We paddled away from the shore a short distance and the Inspector started to fish. After a few casts his line became entangled in some underwater debris so, to free it, we paddled over to the spot and I put my hand over the side into the water but the canoe capsized and both of us were tipped into the lake. The Prime Minister, who was casting his line nearby, saw what happened and drily remarked, "What are you doing Thompson, trying to kill yourself?" I started to swim for the shore but someone dashed over to us in a boat and fished us out of the cold water. The Inspector, who was not a young man, glowered at me. He was most unhappy about the event, however, nothing more than wet clothing and hurt pride was done. When we got back to the cabin a kind member of staff produced trousers and jumpers for us to wear while our wet clothing was taken away to be dried.

Later that evening I had to return to Quebec with a pouch, and was sent on my way with comments about Royal Marines floating in the lake dressed in their blue uniforms. One of my colleagues, Lance Corporal R D Emerson, also fell into the lake when he was delivering a pouch of papers for the Prime Minister. He hung onto the pouch and the papers were not lost, but very wet.

The Quebec Conference having ended, it was time for the main party to pack up for the journey home. Most of the two hundred members of the UK Delegation would be catching the train to Halifax to join the many thousands of Canadian troops onboard the *Queen Mary*.

To embark 15,000 troops in only a few hours from thirty or more special troop trains as they arrived at the dockside must have demanded a high degree of co operation between the military, the *Queen Mary's* staff, and the Canadian Railways.

STAFF CONFERENCE IN CANADA
AUGUST, 1943

THIS IS TO CERTIFY

that .... Mne. W.I. Kitchingham ....

is an authorised member of the United Kingdom Delegation.

The Government of Canada have agreed to accept this document in lieu of a British passport. They have further agreed that the holder is exempt from the normal Canadian immigration regulations. The holder will be freely authorised to disembark in Canada and to re-embark for the United Kingdom.

{Seal of the Offices of the British War Cabinet)

Signature of Holder ....

LONDON, ENGLAND,
    1st August, 1943.

Quebec conference 1943, General pass

Chapter 4
Washington

I was with the small party who were to go with the PM to the USA. We left Quebec by special train in the late afternoon of the 31 August 1943, and had a very enjoyable 700 mile journey southwards to Washington DC. Once again comfortable bunks were prepared in a coach for the night hours.

Next day, during the forenoon, I was doing my turn on guard on the special stores in the baggage car and got into conversation with one of the many US Secret Service Men who were on the train with us. Both of us being interested in weapons, he showed me his hand gun and how to strip it down for cleaning.

We arrived at Washington in the afternoon of the 1 September, and stayed for eleven days, working from the White House where the PM was staying. Our small working party was billeted in the nearby US Marine Corps Barracks.

As during this whole period, both in Canada and now here in the USA, there was plenty of routine courier work to do. However, on the 6th, I had to take some very urgent despatches from the White House to the Prime Minister, who had gone to Boston to deliver a speech at Harvard University. The plan was that I should leave Washington by rail and intercept the PM's train at New York. As I was about to leave the White House, information was received that there had been a serious derailment near Philadelphia causing disruption to train services. This meant that I would not be able to make the rendezvous.

I was, therefore, told to wait while alternative arrangements were made. It was then decided that I should be flown to New York. So I was driven to the local US Army Air Force Base and introduced to the pilot of a two-seater aircraft which was parked near the airfield office block. One of the ground staff assisted me into the harness of a parachute - the pack of which was used as a cushion to sit on in the plane - he then helped me into the rear seat and closed the canopy.

The single engine was rather noisy as we took off and headed northeast for New York, about 220 miles away. I had bought some Hershey bars of chocolate, which had gone rather soft in the heat of Washington, and placed them on the cool side of the canopy to harden up before eating them. Our altitude was not more than a few thousand feet so I had a good view of the countryside below. The pilot pointed out the cities of Baltimore and Philadelphia as we flew along. It was late afternoon when we left Washington and dusk was drawing on as we landed at New York. I was fascinated by the street lights below as we flew over the city.

The American officials had a car and escort waiting at the airfield to take me to the railway sidings where the PM's train was waiting. During the car journey it was explained to me that I would have to change cars, as rapidly as possible, when we reached a certain spot. Upon turning at an intersection with high buildings all round, the car stopped alongside another car waiting at the kerbside. I changed cars and was whisked away in a totally different direction, meanwhile the former car carried straight on. It was now quite dark when I eventually boarded the PM's train in a railway siding, and handed over the pouch to Mr Patrick Kinna, the PM's Clerk, who was waiting for me at the carriage door steps. The train then pulled out of the sidings for the overnight journey to Washington. I had a meal and a chat about the day's events, and settled down for the night journey.

At the White House, late in the evenings after the PM had finished dinner, there would sometimes be a movie show in a small cinema in the basement. I remember sitting in the back row with other members of staff watching the films. We were called on at all hours of the day and night and had to be close by. There was regular contact with the staff of the British Embassy in Washington.

It was quite hot and sticky in Washington and we were wearing our blue uniforms. It would have been more comfortable if we had had our khaki drill uniforms with us. The officers and men of the US Marine Corps made us most welcome, and made facilities at their barracks available to us.

The squirrels running about the lawns and trees in the White House grounds took my fancy, but the White House Guards were quick to warn me that the animals were wild and that I should not think of them as pets.

There had been little time for sightseeing so we took in the sights as we moved about on duty in the official cars. However, my colleague and I had an afternoon and evening off once so we went out to look at the Lincoln Memorial. During our walk three young ladies came up and introduced themselves and we got into conversation with them.

They gave their names and addresses as, Miss Kitty Morgan, Miss Peggy Rapport and Miss Mary Stoneburner, all lived in Washington. A few years later I wrote to them but I did not receive an answer. Perhaps my letters were lost in the mail, the war was still on. After tea we went to a large cinema in the city to see a film. This was the first time I had sat in a cinema where smoking was not allowed. There was, however, an intermission for people to leave the auditorium and go elsewhere for a smoke. Back home one only had to look at the beam of light from the projector to see it shafting through the smoke laden atmosphere. I was not a smoker.

During the morning of the 11 September 1943 we packed our kit bags and prepared the equipment and baggage for the train journey back to Halifax. Later that night, after the PM and his party had boarded the train, we left Washington. Next morning the train stopped at Hyde Park for the Prime Minister and his private party to pay a visit to President Roosevelt at his home.

During the period when the PM was away, we were detailed off in shifts to occupy the PM's coach, which was the rear carriage of the train. This was a well-appointed coach with a lounge section at the rear. A door at the back opened onto an outside observation platform surrounded by iron railings, and steps led down to the track. During the hours we spent occupying the coach we read and talked about things in general. Coffee and snacks were provided by the train's kitchen staff. Later that night, the 12th, with the PM and his party back onboard, the train set off for Halifax arriving in the afternoon of the 14th.

We spent three comfortable nights and three days on this 1000 mile rail journey through the eastern parts of the USA and Canada. The battlecruiser *HMS Renown* was waiting and we soon embarked for the voyage back to Scotland and the Clyde.

One day during the homeward voyage, when I was below on the messdeck, someone came dashing down the messdeck ladder and shouted that Mary Churchill was nearly lost overboard. Mary, one of the PM's daughters, who was accompanying her father as an ADC, was walking up and down the quarterdeck for exercise when a wave broke over the ship's side and caught her unawares, sweeping her along the quarterdeck and washing her up against a guardrail stanchion which saved her from going overboard. One of the Royal Marine sentries on quarterdeck duty rushed to her aid. She had a very lucky escape. My colleague, Ken, and I were usually on duty when it was the practice of the PM to take exercise on the quarterdeck with his daughter, but on this occasion he was in his cabin and unaware of his daughter's narrow escape.

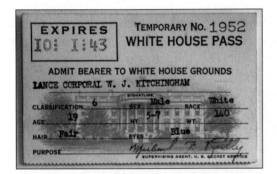

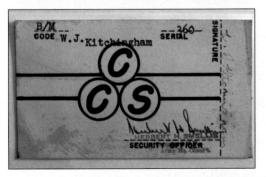

Security passes used in Washington

HMS Renown was one of the Royal Navy's mighty warships. Once at sea she settled down to a good speed with a gentle roll. As we got out into the Atlantic the weather worsened a little and the ship started to pitch slightly. During the crossing the usual changes of course took place as the ship carried out its anti U boat zigzagging routine. When we were in the *Queen Mary* we were many feet above the surface of the sea, whereas here, in *HMS Renown* we were almost hull down at sea level with waves and sea spray breaking over the upper deck at times.

Renown arrived in the Clyde on Sunday morning 19 September 1943.

While the ship's company was called to Divisions for Sunday service on deck, our baggage party was busy getting our stores ashore and onto the special train waiting for us. I was nearby when the PM gave a short address to the ship's officers and men. Then the Special Party left *HMS Renown* for the train and London.

It was late evening when we reached London. We then had a busy few hours. While one group was returning the special stores to offices in Whitehall, other groups were dealing with Col Warden's baggage, and other VIP's bags. We stayed the night in London and returned to Plymouth by rail the next morning.

When I got back to my barrackroom I turned out my kitbag. Moving about and living out of a kitbag, as we had done for the past six weeks, left my kit in a bit of a state. During the trip we had to snap up any opportunity that presented itself to press our uniforms and to wash our underwear. Someone always found a suitable bucket and a length of cord for a clothes line.

A few weeks later I was called to the Adjutant's office and handed a signed photograph of Mr Churchill, with a note saying "A souvenir of your service with the Prime Minister, with his compliments and thanks. Canada and USA 1943". I was also handed a copy of a letter addressed to our Major General from the Prime Minister's office.

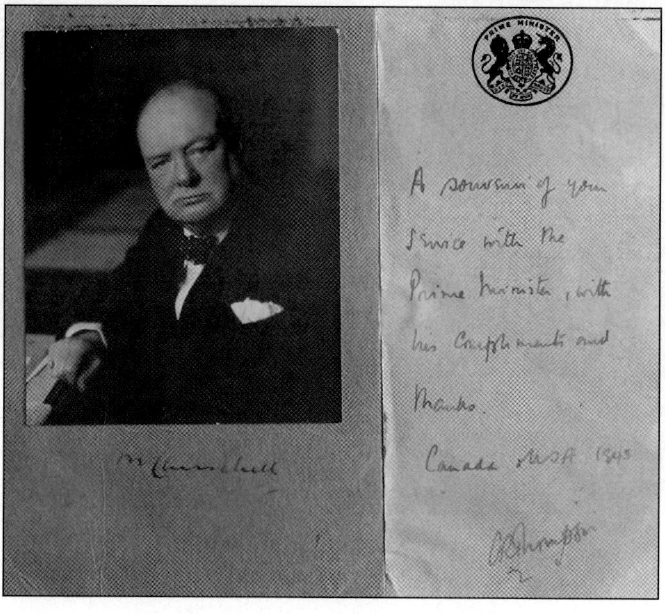
PRIME MINISTER
A souvenir of your
Service with the
Prime Minister, with
his Compliments and
thanks.
Canada USA 1943

COPY.

10 Downing Street,
Whitehall,

20th October, 1943.

Dear Simpson,

I have been meaning to write to you about the Marine Orderlies who were detailed for the Prime Minister during his recent visit to Canada, but as their names were mislaid I had to wait til I got them from Plymouth.
They were:-

Ply.X.2693	L/Cpl	R.D. Emerson
Ply.X.4130	"	W.J. Kitchingham
Ply.X.4153	"	K.N. Wright
Ply.X.4317	"	John Ward

I thought you would be interested to know that they did a remarkably good job. Their duties were varied as in addition to what might be expected from a personal orderly, as a kind of bellhop, they were also required to travel all over parts of Canada and the United States on their own as couriers by air, by car and by boat, not to say train. They always turned up on time and often having surmounted considerable difficulties. I really think they were a remarkable quartette and I am glad that they also had a certain amount of fun, fishing and falling into lakes and other exciting experiences.

I can assure you that the Prime Minister was very well satisfied with their services.

Buckley was in charge of all the Marines for the whole mission for most of the time, and so I did not have much to do with him until after the departure of the main party. He then worked with us and he was the greatest assistance taking on any odd job that wanted doing, and I personally can say that I was most grateful for his help.

Yours sincerely,

signed C.R.Thompson

P.S. I understand the oldest of the L/Cpls was 19½ yrs. What a Corps.

Major-General H.W. Simpson, D.S.O.,R.M.

Typed copy

27

Chapter 5
HMS Jamaica

After attending the Junior Non-Commissioned Officers course at the Depot, Royal Marines, Deal, Kent, where I passed the examination to corporal in December 1943, I returned to Stonehouse Barracks and found that I was to be drafted to the Royal Marine Detachment onboard *HMS Jamaica*. I was to join the ship at the Royal Navy's Home Fleet base at Scapa Flow in the Orkney Islands, just off the north coast of Scotland.

HMS Jamaica was a light cruiser of about 8,000 tons, with a main armament of twelve 6-inch guns in four turrets each of three guns. She also had eight 4-inch high angle guns in four twin mountings, and a number of other smaller anti-aircraft weapons. The ship had a top speed of about 31 knots, a complement of 730 officers and men, and was commanded by Captain J Hughes-Hallett RN.

To travel, as I did, the length of wartime Britain by rail in winter, from Plymouth in Devon to Thurso in Caithness in the north of Scotland, with a change of trains at Crewe to make the connection with the 'Naval Special' from London, was an experience most people, who had to endure such a journey and who remained sober, will always remember. The 600 mile journey took over twenty-four hours, and during the hours of darkness the train was in a state of blackout. As there was little or no heating in the carriages we huddled up in our service greatcoats to keep warm. So, whenever the train stopped at a station there was the ever present wish to get a mug of hot tea and a bun.

It was many years later, when I was in Inverness, that I learned from such retired railway men as Mr K Gordon, who had been a Station Master at Thurso for many years, and Mr Bert Campbell of Inverness, who worked a signal box at Invergordon, of the sterling work of all the staff of the Highland Railway, even in the worst of weather, in keeping the naval rail traffic running, in addition to the ordinary train services, in the north of Scotland during the Second World War.

The railway men in the north referred to the 'Naval Specials' as the 'Jellicoes', but I think this was a term used locally - a left-over from the First World War. Admiral Sir John Jellicoe was Commander-in-Chief of the Royal Navy's Grand Fleet which defeated the German High Seas Fleet at the Battle of Jutland in 1916 and later that year he became the First Sea Lord. The original 'Jellicoes' were coal trains, transporting coal from the mines of South Wales to the Firth of Forth in Scotland for the coal fired boilers of the Royal Navy's Grand Fleet. However, by the time of the Second World War fuel oil boilers had been introduced which put an end to the coal trains - the 'Jellicoes'.

HMS Jamaica, 6-inch Cruiser, in Arctic Camouflage

The 'Naval Specials' which were also first introduced towards the end of the First World War 1914-18, were re-established during the Second World War 1939-45. It was a daily service from London to Thurso and return, and not shown in the published timetables. These trains carried naval personnel north, from the Naval Depots in the south of England, for the ships of the Home Fleet at Scapa Flow. The return journey south was a more happy trip. Men glad to be leaving behind the bleakness of Scapa Flow, and the risks of being at sea in wartime.

The busy Naval Base at Invergordon, which supplied the many ships of the Home Fleet with a multitude of naval stores and supplies, received the freight trains. The operations as a whole placed a severe strain on the railway system much of which, on the Highland Railway, was single track. Additional steam locomotives were used to assist in hauling the trains over those sections of track where the gradients were steep, the highest point being in excess of 1400 feet.

Now, in 1944 on our journey north our train did not enter the station at Inverness but was kept in the sidings while the locomotives and their crews were changed. We then departed in the middle of the night arriving at Thurso, in Caithness at 0730 hours. Here we left the train and were taken to the nearby harbour of Scrabster where we embarked in a steamer for the twenty-two miles crossing of the Pentland Firth to Scapa Flow. The sea had that clean, green look about it, and the wind, which made the crossing rather choppy, felt fresh on my face after the long train journey.

On entering Scapa Flow we went onboard the Accommodation ship, Dunluce Castle, through which all drafts of personnel for the Home Fleet ships, or returning to the mainland, were controlled. There must have been about sixty of us on that draft, most were naval ratings. A petty officer from the Movements Office marshalled us into small groups as our ship's name was called out, I was the only person for *HMS*

Jamaica. All we had to do now was to wait for our individual ship's attendant drifter to collect us.

Suddenly an authoritative voice called out, "Anyone here for *Jamaica*?" I answered, "Yes, me". Thinking, good it will not be long now before I get settled-in on the messdeck, the voice replied, "*HMS Jamaica* has just sailed for Rosyth, you will have to join her there. Get yourself back onto the ferry for Scrabster, here's your travel papers." It was now mid-afternoon, Monday 24 January 1944. There was nothing for it but to get my kitbags and myself onto the ferry and back to the mainland. Another night train journey lay ahead of me, this time south to Rosyth, the Naval Dockyard, just across the Firth of Forth from Edinburgh.

At last I saw the ship, tied up alongside the jetty with dockyard workers already busy carrying out maintenance work of various kinds. I was glad to get onboard and settled-in on the messdeck. The corporal of the mess showed me where to sling my hammock, and indicated an empty clothes locker for my use. Clothes not required for normal ship duties were kept in our kitbags and stowed in the kitbag store.

I soon learned that ship's companies do not like to be onboard when their ship is in dockyard hands. As might be expected, the decks get untidy with pieces of dockyard equipment. Compressed air lines for riveting machines, and electric cables snaked about the place. Sometimes the smell of welding hung on the mess deck air. Nevertheless, the dockyard work had to be carried out for the good of the ship. New equipment such as the latest radar might be fitted.

Life onboard a warship is one of watchkeeping, cleaning messdecks, passages and heads – heads is the naval term for the lavatories. There is the daily administration to be attended to in the various divisional offices, and not least, the feeding of a crew of 730 persons. The routine is controlled by the Quartermaster on the ship's internal loudspeaker system. To attract attention, an announcement is preceded by a bugle call sounded by the duty Boy Bugler, or a 'pipe' from the duty Quartermaster on a boatswain's whistle. Then a voice would give out an order or an instruction. One soon got used to the various 'pipes'.

At 2100 hours each night, there were Commander's Rounds - a general inspection by a senior officer accompanied by other duty personnel, around the messdecks and other parts of the ship to check that all was well.

HMS Jamaica was always in a state of readiness of various degree. At sea it could be 'Cruising Stations' or 'Defence Stations' according to the threat presented by the enemy. These two states required a portion of the ship's armament crews to be closed-up and ready at their guns. 'Action Stations', of course, was all personnel at their action station. During the hours of darkness no outside lights were shown. Lobby doors or passageways leading onto the upper deck were fitted with hooded red coloured lights to help one's eyes adapt to the darkness outside - night adaptation lights as they were known.

The ship's company was made up of Divisions according to branches, for example: seamen, stokers, signalmen and Royal Marines. Each division was divided into Port

Watch and Starboard Watch and these in turn were sub-divided into first part and second part of the watch.

Various spaces throughout the ship housed the ship's company. The officers were allocated small cabins aft, and they had their Wardroom, as a dining room and lounge. The naval ratings' messes were in the forward part of the ship, and the Royal Marines 'Barracks' amidships. Our mess was of ten marines. The table was about thirty inches wide and about ten feet long. It was scrubbed every morning by the duty cooks of the mess. This was a duty we all took turns to do, cleanliness and tidiness being the keynote. Sitting on mess tables was absolutely forbidden. Another thing to remember was to respect other people's messes. After all, this is where we lived, ate our meals, wrote our letters and slept.

Overhead, welded to the deckhead at predetermined distances apart, were stout metal bars from which we slung our hammocks. Each of us had our own hammock space, or billet. This became important when shaking watch-keepers whose duty required them at midnight or at 0400 hours. Day men did not appreciate being shook in the middle of the night by the Corporal of the Gangway, to be asked where was so and so's hammock? I was quite comfortable in my hammock. To keep the head end open I placed a piece of wooden broom handle, about eighteen inches long with a notch at each end across the top cords. At sea, one could see the rolling motion of the ship in relation to the hammocks hanging and swinging from the hammock bars.

A daily issue of rum - two parts water to one part neat rum - was made just before the midday meal for all those entitled.

Being the new boy on the messdeck, I was soon given an outline of what to expect by the old salts - seasoned marines. The big story was the part *HMS Jamaica* played in the Home Fleet's battle with, and the sinking of the German battle cruiser *Scharnhorst* off North Cape in the Arctic on the 26 December 1943 - just four weeks before I joined *HMS Jamaica*.

Now that the *Scharnhorst* had been sunk, there was still the German fast battleship *Tirpitz* to be dealt with. It posed a very serious threat to the convoys as it lay in Altenfjord, Northern Norway, well inside the Arctic Circle. And the Germans had about thirty U-boats stationed in the area. Whilst a number of U-boats were under repair or in dock for maintenance, most were available for operations in these waters.

The protection of these convoys of merchant ships, carrying essential war materials such as tanks; airplanes, munitions, guns and aviation fuel to the Russian port of Murmansk, was one of the many responsibilities of the Home Fleet. It was essential to get these war supplies through in support of the hard pressed Russian war effort.

The seas of the Arctic are well known for the severe gales that blow there, causing very rough seas indeed. We also had to contend with fogs, blizzards and ice. At times, when the weather was very cold, the gun turrets and the ship's upper works were coated in ice from sea spray which froze as soon as it touched exposed metalwork. I did see a few occasions, in the summer, when the weather was calm, a warm sun low in a blue sky and the sea with a gentle swell running. Nevertheless, if a man unfortunately

Proclamation
All Seamen, Wherever Ye May Be,
Greetings: Know All Ye by these Presents
that did on
appear in the Northernmost Reaches of my
Realm, embarked in H.M.S. :
in latitude 66° 33' N. and in longitude
bound for the Dark and Frosty Wastes of
The Land of the Midnight Sun
and did with My Royal Permission,
enter this Dread Region by crossing
The Arctic Circle
by virtue whereof, I, Neptunus Rex, Ruler
of the Raging Main, do hereby declare him
to be a loyal and trusty Bluenose
and do call upon all Icebergs, Polar Bears,
Whales, Narwhals, Sealions and other
Creatures of the Frigid North, to show
him due deference and respect. Disobey
under pain of My Royal Displeasure.
Neptunus Rex
Ruler of the Raging Main.
Commanding Officer.
Queen of His Majesty's Northern Provinces.

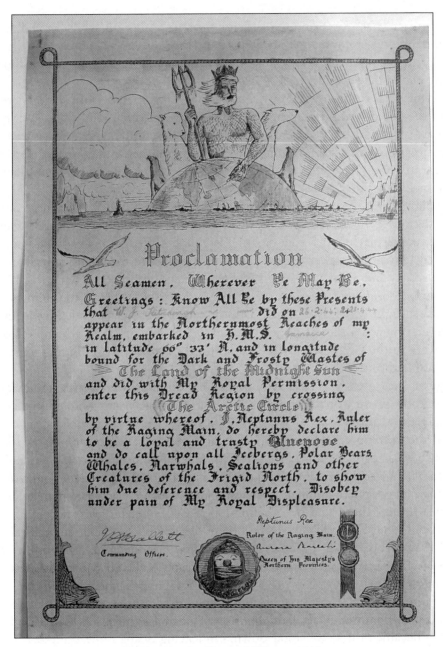

My Bluenose Certificate 26 February 1943

ended up in the sea, and he was not pulled out very quickly, the cold waters would claim him within a few minutes. I have seen the sea temperature recorded at 36 degrees Fahrenheit, (about 2 degrees Celsius) and in general it rarely rose above 40 degrees F (about 5 degrees C). I became a 'Bluenose' on the 26 February 1944, when I crossed the Arctic Circle for the first time. *HMS Jamaica* was in company with the heavy cruiser *HMS Kent,* and the Polish light cruiser *Dragon,* whilst providing 'over the horizon' cruiser cover for convoy number JW57 on its way north to Murmansk. During the previous day a U-boat was sighted some distance away on our portside and we had to take avoiding action.

Whenever I was on watch on the upper deck as a member of the gun's crew on one of the 4-inch twin mountings, and doing my half-hour stint as lookout on the starboard after quarter for enemy submarines or aircraft, I used to be intrigued to see an occasional lone sea bird, gliding effortlessly on the wind close to the ship. The bird, I think could have been a Fulmer, would stay with us for hours, even though we might be 200 hundred miles from land.

At night, when the weather conditions were right, I would occasionally go onto the upper deck to see if the Aurora Borealis, or Northern Lights as they were sometimes called, were displaying. It was fascinating to watch as the streamers of coloured light flickered across the northern sky, at times quite dull then increasing in brilliance.

At sea, day and night, we had our lifebelts with us, an inflatable type which looped over our heads, and side cords to tie around our waists. Attached to the lifebelt was a small red light which would help with rescue at night if we ended up in the sea. However, this was a subject not dwelt on. Curt comments to new members on the mess were to the effect that 'there was no need to worry; ten minutes in the drink and you'd had your lot!'

Our normal dress was navy blue battledress uniforms over warm underclothing and, for those on duty on the upper deck, duffel coats, sheepskin jackets and sheepskin mitts were available.

On the evening of Thursday, 30 March 1944, we sailed out of Scapa Flow in company with the cruisers *HMS Royalist* and *HMS Sheffield;* the escort aircraft carriers *HMS Fencer, Searcher, Pursuer* and *Emperor,* the fleet oilers *Brown Ranger* and *Blue Ranger,* plus a number of screening destroyers. We also had in company one of the large fleet carriers, *HMS Furious.*

Other Home Fleet ships, making up another group, were the battleships *HMS Duke of York* and *Anson;* the cruiser *HMS Belfast,* another large fleet carrier *HMS Victorious* plus their escort destroyers. Two large groups of the Home Fleet were at sea heading north.

We settled down at anti-aircraft cruising stations. Next day the radar must have picked up an enemy aircraft nearby. We had an air raid warning 'Red' and stoodto, but nothing became of it so we stood-down. On leaving Scapa Flow, the Fleet steamed a zigzag course as an anti-submarine measure. Quite a number of U-boats were operating in these waters.

It was a cold, clear and bright morning with a smooth sea and a light wind, when at 0355 hours on the morning of 3 April 1944 we were called to 'Action Stations'. The day before, we had increased speed to 24 knots to get into position.

HMS Jamaica was less than 100 miles from the north coast of Norway with the Home Fleet, escorting the aircraft carriers for a Fleet Air Arm attack on the *Tirpitz* with Barracuda dive bombers. I was in my gun layer's seat of the centre gun in 'Y' turret, the 6-inch turret on the quarterdeck. We always wore our anti-flash gear when at action stations, to protect the exposed skin of our hands, arms and heads from flash burns in the event of enemy shells or bombs hitting our ship.

In the turret we went through our closing-up drill and reported to the bridge that we were ready. It was then a matter of waiting. Our friends down in the shell and cordite handling rooms always wanted to be kept informed of what was happening. Then, as we felt the ship's propellers revolutions increase, we looked at each other. A voice on the Tannoy broke through the silence, "This is the bridge, we are increasing speed to 25 knots and staying on the stern quarters of the fleet carriers whilst they get their strike aircraft airborne. Further information will be given later."

It was not long after that special permission was given by the Captain, for one gun's crew at a time from the 6-inch armament to leave their turret and view the scene around *HMS Jamaica* for a few moments. When it was my turn, I jumped through the small door at the rear of our turret onto the port side of the quarter deck. On our port bow we saw one of the large fleet carriers, with the other escorts of our group spread out in a protective screen. Astern of each ship was their tortured wake, the sea churned up by powerful propellers. I could feel beneath my feet the vibrations of our own four screws as we sped along.

The large fleet carriers were capable of speeds of up to 30 knots and more. Escorts had to keep station but, at the same time, give the carriers sea space for flying operations. The smaller escort carriers were capable of only 15 to 17 knots, and were some miles away with their own escort group.

Whilst we were watching the large fleet carrier, we saw an aircraft moving along the flightdeck with the blur of its single propeller, increasing speed for take-off, but it was unable to get airborne and just flopped into the sea ahead of the bows of the racing carrier. We were then recalled to our action stations inside the turret, and later learned that the aircrew had been lost.

Our Captain had *HMS Jamaica's* radios tuned into the attack aircraft radio wave length and for a short spell the pilots' reports and comments were relayed throughout the ship, but I could not make it out very clearly. As soon as the attack aircraft had returned to their carriers, the whole fleet headed back to Scapa Flow. When we stood-down at 1100 hours we had been closed-up for seven hours.

An hour or so later a cheer went up on the mess deck as we were informed over the Tannoy that the attack had been successful, and that the *Tirpitz* had been hit by a number of bombs. The Fleet had still to be vigilant in case U-boats tried to intercept it on our way back to base.

One of the escort carriers, the *Searcher*, had slowed down for some reason or other, and could not steam faster than 12 knots. *HMS Jamaica* was detached from the fleet and ordered to accompany the carrier back to Scapa Flow, where we arrived on the 6 April, having been at sea for eight days.

As the *Tirpitz* had not been sunk, and was repairable, we left Scapa Flow on the

21st, for another air attack on the 24th, but the strike was cancelled because of bad weather. The 24 April 1944 was my 20th Birthday, and we were at latitude 71.41 north and longitude 13.09 east.

There were a number of U-boat contacts which our destroyer escorts attacked, and *HMS Jamaica* had to make some emergency turns. An incident on our way south brought us to action stations at 0415 hours on the 26th, and next day we had to accompany the escort carrier Emperor to the lee of the Faeroe Islands. *HMS Jamaica* entered Scapa Flow on the 28th.

During the time Royal Navy ships were in Scapa Flow, they would be allocated a drifter from the small fleet of converted fishing boats kept in the Flow to act as 'work maids', by carrying out routine trips for stores, or taking shore leave parties to the fleet canteen and cinema on the heather covered, wind-swept island of Flotta.

Returning to ship in the evenings from Flotta was sometimes quite a show. As might be expected, intership rivalries would break out amongst the shore leave parties as the base canteen beer took charge. Arguments about a particular ship not going to sea very often, or just some silly individual dislike, developed into brawls along the jetty and over the drifters tied up alongside each other.

As there could be a dozen drifters waiting to take personnel back to their ships, there would be a chorus of shouts, such as, "Which is our drifter." Often, we had to clamber over three or four bobbing decks to get to *HMS Jamaica*'s drifter. Whilst the shore patrol was busy with the few 'hard cases', the gentle drunks were usually looked after by their messmates, taken back onboard and laid out on their messdeck to sleep it off, ever thankful next morning for the help they received in getting past the Officer of the Watch. Such acts were rewarded by giving 'sippers' of one's tot of rum. Libertymen were usually inspected on their return to ship to check on their condition.

As a hobby, I made solid model airplanes out of balsa wood kits. We photographed a German model, hanging from a length of black thread, with a view of our ship's guardrails and Scapa Flow in the background which caused quite a stir. We had to explain ourselves to the Naval Censor. I still have the actual photograph.

Whenever *HMS Jamaica* was 'swinging round the buoy' - a naval term for a ship moored in harbour - we sometimes put fishing lines, with hooks baited with silver paper, over the ship's side and caught large sized mackerel. By offering the ship's duty cook some of our catch, the cook in return would fry the fish for our mess. Freshly caught mackerel, cleaned and coated in flour, crispy fried and eaten with a dash of salt, pepper and vinegar, were delicious. However, the Commander did not approve of fishing lines being dangled over the ship's side.

We used to go to Loch Eriboll, a sea loch on the north coast of Scotland, to assist the Fleet Air Arm in their bombing training for their attacks on the *Tirpitz*. A target of the enemy ship was erected in the loch, and shore parties, to simulate conditions the pilots would meet at Altenfjord, would set off smoke canisters when the FAA planes arrived. The *Tirpitz* was such a serious threat to our shipping that she had to be destroyed.

On the 1st and 4th of June 1944, we took onboard more ammunition, little knowing that the Normandy landings were only a few days away. I was on duty as Corporal of the Gangway the morning of the 6th. A buzz had been going round during the night that something big was on. Then we heard it on the BBC radio news that the Allies had landed in Europe. On the 7th and 8th we were at sea with the heavy cruiser *Kent* and eight destroyers escorting the large fleet carriers, *Victorious* and *Furious*, while their aircraft carried out attacks on enemy shipping along the southern coast of Norway.

Back in Scapa Flow, on the 12th, we stored ship and the following day sailed for Greenock to embark a detachment of Norwegian Army personnel, to relieve the small Norwegian garrison stationed on Spitzbergen. We left the Clyde on the 16th but shortly afterwards a shout went up, "Man overboard!" Sadly, despite the ship being turned back, and the off duty watch lining the guard rails to search the area, there was no trace of the man. A head count took place and it was soon discovered that the unfortunate man was one of our naval ratings. No one knew how or why he went overboard.

Our two destroyer escorts *HMS Whelp* and *Wager* joined company with *HMS Jamaica*. There was then a clear run for four days at 18 knots due north for 1500 miles. Past the Arctic Circle, past Jan Mayan Island, and keeping clear of the pack ice we arrived off Spitzbergen on the 20th.

It was quite a fine afternoon as the Captain took *HMS Jamaica* carefully into Advent Fjord and at 1500 hours anchored off Longyearbyen Pier, the ship being kept at a high state of alert in case the enemy should try to surprise us. It was early summer, and the sea passage into Advent Fjord was ice free, however, polar ice was not far away preventing ships from sailing further north. Meanwhile, our destroyer escorts *Whelp* and *Wager* kept watch outside the Fjord.

The ice-covered mountains and the snow on the lower ground presented a picture of grandeur but there was no doubt in my mind that Spitzbergen was a desolate place. However, it provided an excellent base to obtain weather information, and to keep a check on the position and movement of the Arctic ice edge.

Spitzbergen was used by both the Allies and the Germans for that purpose. The weather reports were vital for planning air and naval operations, particularly in the routing of our convoys to Murmansk and Archangel, north or south of Bear Island.

The small population of Norwegians and Russian miners was evacuated in August 1941 by the Allies leaving the settlements deserted. Coal mining equipment was destroyed putting the mines out of production and the German weather station was located and silenced.

A month later the Germans, when they had realized what had happened, landed a small party and started to use Advent Valley, near Longyearbyen, for manned and automatic weather stations, transmitting reports to their base in Northern Norway.

A small force of Norwegians returned to Spitzbergen in May 1942, but the German air force attacked and destroyed the Norwegian's two small ships, inflicting a number of casualties.

Two Royal Navy warships arrived on the 2 July with Norwegian Army reinforcements and tons of supplies. This enabled the Norwegians to re-occupy Longyearbyen, the administration centre of the island, having driven the Germans into the icy wilderness. Royal Navy ships carried out a further re-supply operation in September 1942.

Twelve months later, in September 1943, a strong German naval force comprising the battleship *Tirpitz* and the battle-cruiser *Scharnhorst* with destroyer escorts, left their anchorage in Altenfjord in Northern Norway, and sailed north to Spitzbergen. The Tirpitz entered Icefjord and bombarded the settlements of Longyearbyen and Barentsberg.

Meanwhile, the *Scharnhorst* steamed into Lowe Sound and shelled Sveagruva. Both groups landed troops to search out and kill or capture the Norwegian Garrison who had been putting the German weather stations out of action. The Norwegians knew their island and withdrew into the hinterland until the German ships sailed away, leaving the settlements badly damaged. Catalina flying boats of the Royal Air Force Coastal Command flew regular weather gathering and anti U-boat patrols in the Arctic, including visits to Spitzbergen, and were able to deliver supplies to the garrison, and evacuate wounded.

Now, in June 1944, *HMS Jamaica* arrived with stores and troops to relieve the garrison. There was excitement amongst the Norwegians as they were landed and greeted by their countrymen ashore. I was one of a group of Royal Marines sent ashore to manhandle, up the very stony beach, a variety of stores as they were brought ashore by the ship's boats. Meanwhile, the Captain had sent some working parties ashore to carry out essential repairs to the garrison's meagre facilities. A fire was still smouldering away somewhere inside the workings of the local coal mine. Apparently it started last September when the Tirpitz shelled the place.

When I had a few moments to spare, I scouted around the place and, at the end of the jetty, I came across a pile of half frozen seal skins lying on the ground. One of the Norwegians saw me and said, "Help yourself". I nodded to him and thought to myself, I will take some back onboard. I knew nothing about skins but it seemed better than leaving them there.

A sense of urgency suddenly swept over those members of the ship's company working ashore. A signal from *HMS Jamaica* ordered us back onboard without delay. We had our boats tied to the jetty and quickly got into them for the short trip back to our ship. In the sudden turn of events I had forgotten my seal skins. The time was now 2100 hours but, this far north, there was plenty of daylight at this time of the year, the Midnight Sun being from about the 20 April until about the 23 August.

With all the shore working parties now onboard and accounted for, the Captain took *HMS Jamaica* back to the open sea, joining company with our two escort destroyers, our small force having been at Spitzbergen for about six hours.

A few hours later, as Spitzbergen fell astern of us, some very heavy pack ice was detected about 30 miles away to starboard, but well clear of our course as we steamed south. There was nothing for the relieved Norwegians to do now but settle down for the four day voyage to Scapa Flow. A fleeting contact with a suspected U-boat did not delay us, and we entered the Flow with our destroyer escorts on the 24 June. Our passengers, who were eager to get ashore, were taken off Jamiaca as soon as we anchored.

It was then back to Loch Eriboll for a further period of Fleet Air Arm training on the '*Tirpitz*' target. 14 July 1944 saw us at sea again, for yet another air attack on the repaired *Tirpitz*. Action Stations was sounded just before midnight on the 16th, and we increased speed to 24 knots. The attack went in at about 0230 hours on the 17th, by aircraft from three fleet carriers, the *Formidable*, *Indefatigable* and the *Furious*. The sea escort was provided by the battleship *HMS Duke of York*, the heavy cruiser *Devonshire*, the light cruiser *Bellona*, eight destroyers and *HMS Jamaica*; a strong force of fifteen Royal Navy warships. This was a much faster run, six days for the round trip instead of eight as was the case in the early April operation. But the risk of U-boat attack was very serious as there was no slow moving convoy in the area to draw off the enemy submarines.

Long range Catalina aircraft of the Royal Air Force Coastal Command were covering the Fleet's returning course and, on the 18th, sank three U-boats. However, the Fleet entered Scapa Flow on the 19th in the knowledge that the *Tirpitz* was still afloat.

13 August 1944 saw *HMS Jamaica* sailing the short distance from Scapa Flow to Loch Ewe, on the west coast of Scotland and later that day the Captain received some Russian Officers for a meeting in his cabin. A convoy of thirty-three laden freighters was forming, and would be identified as Convoy JW59. The close escort would comprise two escort carriers, the *Vindex* and *Striker*, seven destroyers, four sloops, two frigates, five corvettes and, of course, *HMS Jamaica*. In all, fifty-four ships sailed in convoy on the 15th for the 1900 miles voyage to Kola Inlet at nine knots. Although we had 6-inch guns they were no match for the Tirpitz if she came out after the convoy, but our consolation was that we knew some ships of the Home Fleet with big guns were covering us from astern, out of sight over the horizon.

Our slow voyage was not without incident. On the 17th we were north of Scapa Flow and ran into banks of fog. So we streamed our fog buoy on a long wire rope astern until we were clear of the fog. The sight and splashing of the fog buoy in the sea would warn the ship following us of our position and help it to keep station.

We were well inside the Arctic Circle, south-east of Jan Mayan Island, when one of the escorts reported a contact. A U-boat had intercepted the convoy, and no doubt there were others on patrol looking for us. To add to our vigilance an enemy aircraft had also appeared and no doubt the pilot radioed our position back to his base.

On Sunday the 20th we sighted the *Archangel*. It was formerly the Royal Navy battleship *HMS Royal Sovereign* and now transferred to the Russian Navy. She was on passage from Scapa Flow to Murmansk with a dozen small craft. There was quite a sea running and the *Archangel*, being a battleship, was weathering the gale, but it was quite obvious the small mine sweepers were having a horrible time. It was said on the messdeck that a couple of the small sweepers had foundered during the night. Next morning, the 21st, an enemy submarine sank one of our escorts, the sloop *Kite*, a few miles away from us on our starboard quarter. Only nine men out of the ship's company of nearly 200 were rescued.

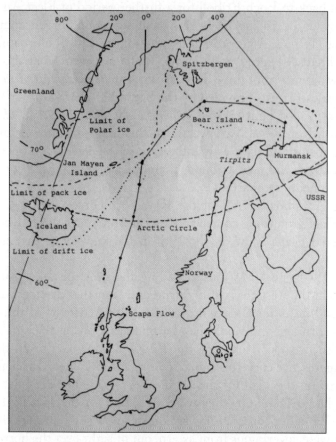

The ten day, l900 mile track of Arctic Convoy JW59 of 33 loaded freighters from Loch Ewe to Murmansk, 15 to 25 August 1944. The close escort was provided by escort aircraft carriers *Vindex* and *Striker* with 7 destroyers, 5 corvettes, 4 sloops, 2 frigates and HMS *Jamaica*.

The convoy had passed north of Bear Island by the 22nd, and was on a southeasterly course for Kola Inlet. At eight and a half knots we would not reach it for another two days.

The bugle call for anti-aircraft stations, from the Tannoy, cut through the mess deck noise. As my mess mates and I rushed for our twin 4-inch, the starboard after mounting on the upper deck, we passed some of the damage control teams making their way between decks. Our NCO in charge of the mounting shouted at us, "Come on, chop chop." I got into my gun layer's seat on the left side of the guns, and the trainer was in his seat on the right side. The first shell was put on the fuse setting tray, and our NCO reported, "Closed up." An order came back to "Follow director."

As the trainer brought the mounting to a bearing of about Green 70 degrees, I noticed the gun elevation indicator was at a low angle, so I looked through my gun sight but could not see a target. It was a cold, dull day with low overcast cloud. It was evident that the radar and gunnery director were tracking an aircraft. Suddenly it broke through the low cloud and I saw a slow moving aircraft less than 1000 yards away moving from left to right with a slight inclination towards us. The voice of our NCO said, "Come on, let's get it right first time." But a few seconds later the aircraft banked to its left opening the range and made off into the cloud cover. Shortly after we stood down an enemy Blohm and Voss 138 flying boat was shot down by an aircraft from one of our escort carriers.

In the afternoon I was walking up and down the port waist with two friends to get some exercise when one of the escort destroyers near *HMS Jamaica* suddenly gave two shrill blasts on its siren. We watched as she turned away from us and increased speed, back tracking along our course. Later that day a U-boat was reported sinking some distance astern of us.

Meanwhile the Home Fleet carriers and sea escorts had sailed from Scapa Flow and were off the Norwegian coast for yet another FAA attack on the *Tirpitz*.

Ten days after leaving Loch Ewe the thirty-three freighters of convoy JW59 were in Kola Inlet, and made their way to the Russian port of Murmansk to unload their many tons of cargo. The constant threat of German air attack in the Murmansk area meant that our anti-aircraft guns had to be at a degree of readiness. The day after we arrived, *HMS Jamaica* and the other escort ships moored in Vaenga Bay received an air raid warning 'Red' which sent the anti aircraft guns' crews scurrying to their stations. Tension eased when no enemy aircraft ventured near us and we stood down.

Shore leave was restricted to a few hours a day, and only to a small part of the ship's company at a time. When my Part of Watch was granted shore leave I went for a walk with a few other marines, along a hard packed earth road to get some exercise. We came upon a group of Russian service men and women whom we understood belonged to an anti-aircraft battery and searchlight unit, part of the Russian defences of the area. We were not able to speak each other's language but they were pleased to see us, and obviously knew all about the convoys. We exchanged uniform badges and money. I still have the Russian badges and money given to me.

It was now time for the return voyage. We sailed p.m. on the 28 August 1944 as close escort to the nine merchant ships of convoy RA59A bound for the United Kingdom. The hours on watch dragged, we were just wallowing along at about eight knots. However, the convoy was routed south of Bear Island which would shorten the voyage time.

On the 2 September we were still well inside the Arctic Circle and heading south when a U-boat was detected near the convoy. It was promptly set upon by our escorts and sunk. The voyage ended without further incident and *HMS Jamaica* parted company with the convoy, entering Scapa Flow on the 5 September 1944.

A couple of days later we went to Rosyth Dockyard while a check was made on some of our equipment. We had sailed 25,000 miles in Arctic waters during the last six months and an inspection was necessary. We returned to our base at Scapa Flow on the 14th.

Then on the 26th *HMS Jamaica* sailed to Greenock to take onboard stores and a few Norwegian Army personnel for Spitzbergen. Two destroyers, the *Orwell* and *Obedient* were assigned as our escorts. So, on the 30 September 1944 we sailed from Greenock for Spitzbergen once again. Next day, the 1 October, we were not many miles north-east of the Faeroes when an enemy aircraft was sighted ahead of us, but it flew off into the far distance. However, next day an underwater contact was reported, possibly a U-boat but we kept sailing on at 20 knots. The sighting of another enemy aircraft on the 3 October kept us on our toes.

As we approached Spitzbergen on the morning of the 4th the weather was feeling much colder, and the sea temperature was recorded as 36 degrees Fahrenheit - about 2 degrees Celsius. The Captain brought *HMS Jamaica* into the anchorage at 1250 hours and work commenced without delay. Stores were landed, and I was again one of the shore party. Meanwhile, the transfer of the small number of Norwegians took place. Then at 1800 hours we were glad to be on our way again, scuttling along at a brisk 23 knots for Scapa Flow, 1500 miles to the south. Three days later, the 7th, we entered Scapa without any incidents en route.

A buzz went around the messdecks that we were going into dockyard hands at Portsmouth. Sure enough, we left Scapa Flow on the 9th, and entered Portsmouth harbour a.m. on the 11 October 1944. The next two days were spent in emptying the ship's magazines, putting all the ammunition into lighters which had come along side for the purpose.

Arrangements were made between the ship and the city of Bristol, which had offically adopted the ship, for the ship's company to visit the city. So, on the 18 October we set off by train and had a nice day at Bristol, being entertained in the Colston Hall. *HMS Jamaica* presented the city with a silver casket and the battle ensign worn by the ship during the *Scharnhorst* action in December 1943.

HMS Jamaica now commenced a period of refit, and the ship's company was reduced in numbers. The Royal Marine Detachment left *HMS Jamaica* at 0900 hours on the 27 November 1944, and caught a train with reserved compartments, which the Railway Transport Officer, RTO, had arranged for us for the journey back to Stonehouse Barracks.

Chapter 6
Yalta

In early January 1945 I was in Stonehouse Barracks, having left *HMS Jamaica* two months earlier, when I was instructed to report to the Orderly Room Sergeant Major who informed me that I was under a temporary draft order, with a number of other ranks, to form a special party under the Adjutant, Major Buckley. I guessed this was probably another conference trip. We had to be ready to leave in about 48 hours' time, so we bustled about getting our innoculations up-to-date, drawing new uniforms and kit as necessary. Our total party consisted of 2 officers and 57 other ranks, and would be known as 'Party Argonaut', but we had no idea of our destination.

On the 15 January 1945 we caught the morning train from Plymouth North Road station arriving in London in the late afternoon, and were accommodated for the night in the Union Jack Club, which was close to Waterloo Railway Station. Next morning we collected, packed and marked official stores from offices in Whitehall, and collected VIP personal baggage as required. We took it all to Addison Road railway station, loaded the special train and posted Royal Marine guards - during the war years this West London railway depot had been the scene of many special train departures. For having worked so hard during the day permission was then given for those who so wished to 'have a quick wet' at one of the pubs close to the station.

At about 2200 hours the Conference personnel started to arrive, and we acted as guides and baggage parties to assist them into the railway coaches as allocated in the accommodation list. At the time I had not given much thought to the very detailed planning and organisation required for these conferences.

It was not until many years later that I discovered that a lady, by the name of Mrs Joan Bright Astley, nee Bright, working for General Sir Hastings Ismay, was the leading light in these arrangements. I had the pleasure of meeting her in London in February 1991. She had written a very interesting book with the title "The Inner Circle, A View of War at the Top", in which she gives accounts of the detailed 'housekeeping' arrangements required for the British Delegations at these wartime, Big Three conferences.

At about midnight a check was made that all was well, and the train pulled out of the station at 0030 hours on the 17 January 1945. Liverpool was reached in the forenoon and we had a busy time getting all the personnel, baggage and official stores onboard the *Franconia*, a Cunard liner of 20,000 tons. Vehicles and RAF equipment, which would be required at Yalta, had been loaded earlier. It was about 1400 hours on the 17th when we sailed out of Liverpool into the Irish Sea and headed north.

To avoid U-boats the *Franconia* was routed round the North of Ireland where we ran into a fierce gale. The seas were so rough that the Captain had to reduce the ship's speed. The Royal Marines were accommodated in the after section, and when the ship was pitching and tossing we could hear the rumbling of the propeller as the ship's stern rose almost out of the sea. I saw some very seasick people during this period, and I mean very seasick. Afterwards, some said that they felt like dying. I must say that the gale was a bad one. I had been in some violent storms when serving onboard *HMS Jamaica*, so I felt sorry for them. Those of us who were fit enough kept an eye on the sick until the weather improved. I was lucky in being a fairly good sailor.

We had onboard several hundred conference personnel, and there were more at Malta, who would be flown on to the Crimea when the Combined Chiefs of Staff meeting at Malta ended. I later learned that about 700 persons would be involved. There were Royal Air Force ranks to service the aircraft, which would fly daily from the United Kingdom to the Russian airfield at Saki; Royal Army Service Corps drivers and mechanics for our vehicles, Royal Naval officers and ratings including WRNS for the vital communications network, and there were civilian staff from various departments of Whitehall.

The *Franconia*, which was normally fitted out as a troopship, had had a number of internal alterations made to enable her to act as the British Delegation HQ Ship when we arrived in Sevastopol Harbour. Apparently the total devastation of the Crimea area made it impossible for all the personnel of the British and American Delegations to be accommodated ashore. The American ship was the *Catoctin*.

We passed Gibraltar on the 23rd, and arrived in Grand Harbour, Malta on the 25th, eight days since leaving Liverpool. The gale had delayed *Franconia* quite a few hours. However, there was soon a flurry of activity as personnel and stores for the Combined Chiefs of Staff meeting to be held on the Island prior to the Conference at Yalta went ashore.

This was my first visit to Malta. Early next morning from high up on the upper deck of *Franconia* we had a good view of Grand Harbour. There were some warships at anchor and a number of small craft scurried about on the calm waters. On the shore side we could see the Custom House steps where people were being landed, and Valletta rising in the background. A friend who was on the upper deck with me said, "Come round to the other side, you can see the Ohio tied up alongside the wall."

Out of a convoy of fourteen merchant ships with Royal Navy escort ships, Ohio, a merchant tanker with over 10,000 tons of fuel oil onboard was one of only five cargo ships to reach beseiged Malta in August 1942. Malta was out of fuel and in dire need of supplies. King George VI in recognition of the heroism of its people during World War Two awarded Malta the George Cross.

We left Grand Harbour at noon on the 26th. The Mediterranean Sea was not at all warm and sunny as we sailed east and then north into the Aegean Sea. It was during this period that we were given briefing sessions to ensure that we were alert to what lay ahead when we got ashore. One of the interpreters gave a talk on the Russian outlook and their way of life, and reminded us of the terrible suffering of the

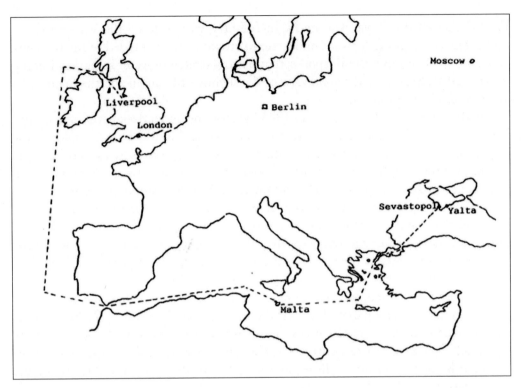

The 4,500 mile track of the Cunard Liner *SS Franconia* for the period 17 to 30 January 1945 from Liverpool to Sevastopol via Malta with personnel, vehicles, stores and equipment for The British Delegation at the Yalta Conference February 1945

Russian Peoples. The ship's doctor, in his turn, advised us on health and local diseases in the area. He also warned that the change in food and drink might have a reaction on us and that we should pay attention to good hygiene. The officer from the Military Intelligence Service, Major Boddington, was at pains to ensure that all ranks realised the importance of being security minded at all times, and when we got to the Yalta area he gave us further individual instructions, of a rather special and detailed nature.

During our passage through the Dardanelles and the Bosphorous all ranks, from the generals down to the other ranks, had to wear civilian clothing as the exact attitude of the Turkish Government to our presence in these waters was not known. Someone had provided enough civilian clothes for the male and female service personnel onboard, albeit rather ill fitting.

As we went through the Dardanelles, Major Buckley, our detachment officer, gave the Royal Marines a lecture on the Gallipoli Campaign, which was fought in World War One and where casualties had been very high. He made special reference to the operations of the Royal Marine Brigade and the Plymouth Battalion and pointed out to us the beaches and prominent features of the land.

It was interesting to see the actual place of the campaign, particularly as it was one of the notable events in our Corps history. It was here, in 1915, that Lance Corporal

W R Parker, of the Royal Marine Light Infantry, was awarded the Victoria Cross for his bravery in going forward under fire to attend to the wounded in the trenches.

As we went through the Bosporus, that narrow stretch of water in Turkey leading into the Black Sea, we had a good view of the skyline of Istanbul and the many villas and houses along the coast.

On the morning of the 30 January 1945 I was on the upper deck with some friends looking at the horizon ahead. The weather was cold and murky but we could see the high ground of the Crimea, looking rather grey, coming into view as the *Franconia* approached the steeply rising coastline. About an hour later we were met by a Russian ship and escorted through the Russian minefields into Sevastopol harbour.

It was early afternoon and snowing as we berthed, a 4500 mile voyage from the UK. The snow and icy conditions made the unloading of our vehicles and stores rather slow going. It took a couple of days, much longer than planned. The Royal Air Force stores went first as they had to set up an aircraft servicing unit at Saki airfield some fifty miles to the north, then the Royal Army Service Corps vehicles were put ashore. In the meantime, ship-to-shore communications were established.

I was in the advance party which left the ship in a small convoy of RASC vehicles and headed for Yalta, some fifty miles to the south east of Sevastopol. The main party would follow next day. A rear party would be left onboard the ship to provide patrols and guards for the sensitive offices, and orderlies to deal with the disposal of the secret waste.

We were travelling at the rear of our vehicle convoy. It was a cold day and I was glad to be in a comfortable Humber 4 X 4 Box Staff car driven by an RASC driver. I was wearing our normal blue uniform with bright polished buttons, and a peak cap with a red band round the crown. The driver was in khaki.

Winding our way from the harbour area through the streets of Sevastopol we saw at close quarters the nightmare devastation the war had brought to this area, the city was in ruins. At one point the driver said to me, "Look over there, nodding to the right side of the street as we drove past a group of prisoners. They were poorly dressed and had strips of cloth wrapped around their legs. They looked a sorry sight as they shuffled along, each pushing a small wheelbarrow loaded with chunks of building stone. I said, "The poor bastards"

When we got out of the city onto the open road to Yalta we came upon a large area of ground on both sides of the road. The weathered rims of hundreds of shell, mortar and bomb craters, interlaced with each other, not a single square yard of earth seemed to have escaped being churned up by explosives. Bits of jagged, twisted rusted metal were to be seen sticking out of the ground. Without doubt there had been some very vicious fighting here between the Russian and German armies.

About half an hour after leaving the ship the convoy stopped. Up front one of the drivers was unhappy with his vehicle. Some wheel nuts had worked loose, so all the drivers were instructed to check their vehicles and tighten any loose wheel nuts. We were alright with the Humber. Later on one of the leading small vehicles had a steering link work loose, and it ended up in the ditch. No one was hurt and the vehicle was recovered next day.

The road wound its way up into the mountains round a fair number of rather severe hairpin bends, over the Baidar Gap at a height of about 3000 feet, and down to the Black Sea coast where it was a little warmer. Russian sentries had been posted along the whole route, about 200 yards apart or closer and certainly within sight of each other. They acknowledged us as we waved to them in passing, some of the sentries were young women.

We were making reasonable time and a stop was made to have some sandwiches which the ship's galley staff had prepared for us. Our blessings descended on the head of some very thoughtful person who had had the foresight to include in our stores a supply of cans of army self-heating cocoa and soups. So, within a few minutes we were having a hot drink.

This stop, however, created a small incident with a Russian sentry who was close to where we stopped. I had punched two holes in the top of the can near the rim, prised off the small cap to expose a short fuze and lit it. The sentry obviously took a dim view of this and got agitated, pointing his rifle at the can but, as we were standing around the heating cans and used sign language to calm him down, he decided that all was well. So we heated up a can of hot cocoa for him and made a friend out of a comrade.

We drove on without any further incidents. It was late afternoon as we entered the built-up area of Alupka. Here there were villas surrounded by high garden walls. Shrubs and Cypress trees dotted the area.

Russian service personnel waved to us from the first floor windows of some of the habitable houses as we made our way to the British Delegation accommodation which had been prepared in two Sanatorium buildings. It was obvious the Russians had worked very hard to repair, decorate and furnish the buildings in time for the conference. The war had made its mark.

We were met by the British Delegation Administration Officer, Miss Joan Bright, who took us to our rooms which were on the ground floor. I was in a room with six other Royal Marines. She came back shortly afterwards and introduced a rather attractive looking Russian young lady who spoke English, and said that she was the administration liaison officer for our stay, and could be contacted in the hallway of the main building if we had any problems. I pointed out that we needed haircuts and asked if a barber was available. The Russian lady, who was soon nicknamed the 'Russian Princess' by us, said that there was one in a room near the bath-house. Imagine our surprise when we discovered, later, that both the barber and the bath house attendants were women.

As some of our detachment were soon to be required for duty, we quickly unloaded our kit from the vehicles, arranged our bed spaces and made a reconnaissance of our surroundings.

The building was a sturdy castle-like villa with a ground floor and an upstairs.

The fairly large entrance hall had a big fireplace at each end, in which cheerful log fires were kept burning. This was the Vorontzov Palace. Here, there was accommodation for Mr Churchill, his daughter Sarah, a number of close aides, a few senior government officials and service chiefs. Rooms were set aside as principal offices, and there was a large room for conferences. The Map Room was set up close to the Prime Minister's suite.

The Vorontsov Palace had escaped damage from the Germans. It was said to have been the headquarters of the invading German Army Commander, General von Mannstein - before the Russians forced a very rapid retreat on him - and that it had been promised to him as a permanent residence after the war, by Hitler.

I was one of the Corporals with a small group of Royal Marines on duty as guards for Mr Churchill in the Palace. The watchkeeping routine was worked out and the first Marines on duty were posted. The remainder went for a meal and an early night in bed. There was, of course, a heavy guard of Russian military personnel around the Palace, and in the Yalta area generally.

When I awoke early next morning and pulled my bedding back I saw a few small red stains on the sheets, so I took a closer look. A sleepy voice from the next bed inquired, "What's the matter?" "I am not sure," I replied, "but I've got blood spots on my sheets." Then I remembered the doctor's lecture on the ship and said, "I think we've got bed bugs!" That did it! The other members of the room were out of bed in a flash and checking their own beds. Yes, we had bed bugs, and we would not be alone. The PM and just about everyone in both the British and American Delegations had the same experience.

We stripped our beds and took them outside. Paper was obtained, rolled into small torches and the flame passed over every part of the metal bed frame and springs. Next, the seams and button discs of the mattresses were thoroughly picked over, squashing any of the small flat pests that were found. Later, some cans of AL63, a DDT delousing powder appeared, so we gave our kit, beds and the floor of our room a dusting.

No more bugs. We also gave a few cans of the powder to our very helpful Russian domestic staff, who were most grateful. I am sure we made some more friends. Two Marines were sent to assist the PM's butler, Mr Frank Sawyers, and the other senior officers' attendants, deal with the VIP beds.

Monday, 5 February 1945, saw the tempo of activity increase as meetings were held at the various locations. The Americans were at the Livadia Palace, about thirty minutes by car away from us, and the Russians were in the Yusupov Palace at Koreiz, rather closer, about fifteen minutes away.

Early one evening, after a meeting had been held at our location and the personages had left, I went into the conference room to make our usual special check before anyone else. On the floor by the legs of a chair, where one of the Russian officers had been sitting, I saw a brief case. Without anyone noticing me I took it to one of our senior government officers. As he took it away to his office, upstairs, he instructed me to let him know if anyone inquired after it.

I was standing in the main entrance hall, by one of the log fires, when he returned it to me about fifteen minutes later and said that I was to give it back to whoever asked for it, and to let him know who it was. Within a few minutes a Russian officer came through the main door. I watched him as he went to the Russian Receptionist on duty, a male in civilian clothing who was sitting at a desk by the other log fire, at the far end of the hall, and noticed them speaking in very low tones. At this point the Russian young lady interpreter, whom the Royal Marines had struck up a good rapport came into the hall, walked up to the receptionist's desk and was immediately engaged in conversation with the two males. She nodded to the uniformed officer walked over to me and, with a nice smile, inquired if a brief case had been handed in. I said that one had and picked it up from the floor behind me whereupon the officer, on seeing the case, nodded that it was his. She asked me if anyone had opened it. I said that I had not opened the case, nor had I seen anyone look inside it. Thanking me, she took the case and strode back across the hall and handed it to the officer who had a quick look inside. He seemed satisfied, they exchanged a few words and he sped out of the main door into a waiting car.

The evening of the 10th was a very busy period for us. The Yalta Conference having ended, the PM hosted a dinner for President Roosevelt and Marshal Stalin in the Vorontzov Palace. Just before the appointed time sixteen of us under our officer, Major Buckley, were formed up in the large entrance hall as a guard of honour for the guests when the place became alive with civilian clothed Russian and American Secret Service men. Mr Roosevelt was expected first, and Marshal Stalin a few minutes later, but events did not keep to the timetable. While we waited, Mr Churchill walked over to Major Buckley and expressed his satisfaction with the work of the detachment.

Suddenly, a number of Kremlin Guards in smart uniforms marched into the hall and placed themselves in front of us, like a screen, but we elbowed our way between them to the front again just as Marshal Stalin walked through the main doorway.

Although we were standing to attention, I was able to watch what was happening about four or five paces away to my right front. Mr Churchill walked towards the entrance and greeted his guest. Stalin removed his own overcoat, and Mr Churchill attempted to assist him in hanging it on the coat stand, by the door, but an aide quickly moved in and completed the task.

The PM then escorted Stalin towards the banqueting room and, in passing just in front of us, indicated and said, "Some of my Marines, representatives of one of the finest Corps in the World." The Marshal replied, through his interpreter, "I know well of them, they are clearly highly trained." A few moments later Mr Roosevelt, in his wheelchair and not looking at all well, arrived saying, "Sorry I am rather late." The dinner party was now complete, the banqueting room door was closed and guards took up their posts. For the duration of the dinner I was on duty at the doorway through which the waiters carried the numerous courses. One of the President's Secret Service men was also stationed at this door. We chatted the time away as we watched course after course being taken in to the diners. The menu offered about twenty choice items of food. I particularly noticed a whole fish, about three feet long from head to tail and looking very appetising, being carried in on a large oval salver, but I was very surprised when the waiter returned to see that only a few pieces had been cut from the middle of the fish.

Earlier, during the afternoon, I was in and out of the banqueting room a number of times, doing my security rounds, and saw the domestic staff preparing the large round dining table.

At each place setting numerous items of silver cutlery were laid out, and there was an array of elegant wine glasses ranging from champagne flutes; tulips, cognac and liquor glasses down to the very small vodka glasses, which held no more than a couple of thimbles full of vodka.

When the dinner came to an end and the diner's left - the American Secret Service man went with his President. I entered the room, just as the waiters started to clear away the cutlery and china, and made a check at each chair place to see if anything had been left behind. The smell of good food, drinks and cigar smoke hung in the air.

At the place where Mr Churchill had been sitting the contents of an ash tray were attracting the attention of the waiters, however, the Russian in charge of the domestic staff took the cigar ends as souvenirs. Other souvenirs of such a momentous occasion were also spirited away.

This meeting turned out to be the last time these world leaders would dine together as a threesome - the ailing President Roosevelt died two months later at Warm Springs, Georgia, in the United States of America on the 12 April 1945, a few weeks before the war in Europe came to an end.

We re-embarked in *Franconia* on the 12 February after saying goodbye to our friends at Alupka who had taught us a few words of Russian during our short stay. The previous day, Sunday, had been spent packing up all the equipment and sending it back to the ship.

It was some days later, after the Prime Minister and his party flew out from Saki airfield, before the RAF equipment from the airfield and the vehicles could be loaded. During this period escorted visits were arranged to places of interest around Sevastopol. Some RASC vehicles were made available and I went with a small group which made a stop at Balaclava, about eight miles south of Sevastopol. Here was a smooth depression in the open grassy countryside - the site of the charge of the Light Brigade on the 25 October 1854, during the Crimean War.

Onboard General Sir Hastings Ismay addressed our detachment; he thanked us and explained the importance of the mission to Yalta. And later we had a warm expression of thanks from the ship's Staff Captain.

At Mr Churchill's base in the Vorontzov Palace at Alupka we had had a very busy time. Our small detachment provided sentries for the Prime Minister, his Map Room, conference rooms and important offices. Security patrols within the building were also arranged. My usual place had been in the main entrance hall where I witnessed

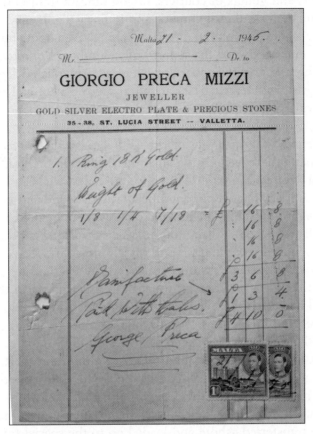

Receipt for our wedding ring purchased in Valletta, Malta, February 1945.

Security Passes used at Yalta Conference February 1945

the daily comings and goings of couriers, liaison officers from both the Americans and Russians, and many senior diplomatic and military dignitaries.

Seven courier trips a day in each direction, taking seven hours for the ninety mile round trip, from our location to the support offices onboard *Franconia* at Sevastopol were required. There were regular courier trips to the American delegation at Livadia Palace and the Russian Headquarters at the Yusupov Palace at Koreiz. The Prime Minister's four orderlies, all Lance Corporals, worked in pairs and had their time fully occupied.

It was snowing on the morning of the 17 February as *Franconia* sailed out of Sevastopol Harbour, the Soviet Union's main naval base in the Black Sea, for Malta and home to the United Kingdom. When we arrived at Malta, a number of senior staff officers and important government officials disembarked and flew on to the UK.

As the ship was at Malta for a couple of days we were granted a few hours shore leave each day. It was when I was ashore in Valetta, walking up the steps from the harbour to have a look around that I found myself in St Lucia Street and came upon a jeweller's shop which gave me the opportunity to buy an 18 carat gold wedding ring instead of the utility rings available in the UK. Before leaving on this trip, Patricia, my fiancee, and I had decided to be married on my return. We had looked at wedding rings in Plymouth, but I had not yet bought one. I knew the size to get, one to fit my little finger. I still have the receipt, dated 21 February 1945.

We left Malta on the 23rd, and called at Gibraltar on the 26th. Royal Navy escort ships joined us as we sailed next day for Liverpool where we arrived on the evening of the 5 March 1945 without any incidents.

Next morning the Conference personnel with their baggage, special stores and equipment were transferred ashore and loaded on to the special train. We departed Liverpool docks at 1015 hours, arriving in London at 1630 hours. That evening we were busy returning stores to various Government offices in Whitehall, including boxes to the War Cabinet Offices.

Once again we spent the night in the Union Jack Club, and next morning, the 7 March 1945, we returned by train to Stonehouse Barracks, Plymouth.

Chapter 7
HMS Duke of York

The day following my return to Stonehouse Barracks from the Yalta trip I saw on the noticeboard that I was to join the Royal Marine Detachment onboard the battleship *HMS Duke of York*, on the 23 March. The ship was at Liverpool having been in the Gladstone Dock for a refit.

The draft was given a few days pre-embarkation leave, so Patricia and I decided to be wed as soon as it could be arranged. We were married by special licence on the 13 March 1945 in the Parish Church of St Margaret, Rainham, Kent, and returned to Plymouth after spending a few days in London at the Cadogan Hotel. Patricia would continue living with her parents until I returned. The war was still on, and there was no clear end to it in sight.

Our draft of one Colour Sergeant and twenty three Royal Marines arrived at Liverpool on the morning of the 23rd by train from Plymouth. By 1030 hours we were onboard the ship and took our places on the mess deck with the other members of the detachment.

HMS Duke of York was a battleship, capable of a top speed of about 28 knots, with a displacement of nearly 40,000 tons. The ship had a main armament of ten 14-inch guns, and a secondary armament of sixteen dual purpose 5.25-inch guns. She was fairly bristling with close range anti-aircraft guns, Pom-Poms, Bofors and Oerlikons. The Admiralty was well aware that Japanese Air Force pilots press their attacks on ships to the limit, even to suicide attacks by crashing their planes onto the ships.

We had a crew of over 1600 officers and men, which included the Royal Marine detachment of 300, quite a community, many of whom I had never met. The Royal Marines messes were on the main deck, amidships, and I was Corporal of number 112 mess on the portside.

The ship had the usual facilities of a large warship. A dental surgery, sick bay with operating theatre, a quiet Chapel, a laundry, stowage spaces, washrooms and heads. The galley was always busy, and the bakery produced crusty fresh bread and rolls daily.

The King and Queen visited the ship on the 27th, which resulted next day at noon of 'Splice the Mainbrace' - a double ration of rum for those entitled, and warmly accepted.

Upon leaving Liverpool we went to Scapa Flow for a short period for the new crew to settle down and get used to running the ship. We left the bleakness of Scapa Flow on the 25 April 1945 for the warmer climate of the Mediterranean Sea and Malta to complete our work-up. One of our three sister ships, *HMS Anson*, had now joined us. She also was on her way to the Far East to join the British Pacific Fleet.

Our other two sister ships, the *HMS Howe* and *HMS King George V*, were already in the Pacific War area engaged in operations against the Japanese.

The fifth battleship of our class, the *HMS Prince of Wales*, had been attacked and sunk along with the battlecruiser *HMS Repulse* and four destroyers, in the South China Sea on the 10 December 1941, by bombs and torpedoes from Japanese aircraft.

We arrived in Grand Harbour, Malta on the 2 May. It was the first time for most of the ship's company to be in the 'Med', a new experience far different from that of being in the Arctic. The weather was nice and warm compared with Scapa Flow, and everyone enjoyed a good run ashore in Valetta.

During the next few days, a buzz went round the messdecks that Germany was going to surrender. There was great excitement when it was actually confirmed. VE Day was celebrated on the 8 May.

A sizeable fleet was in Grand Harbour, and the Maltese Police were very tolerant with ships companies on shore leave. Although the lads went ashore to enjoy themselves and let off steam, too much alcohol invariably led to arguments and brawls. In fact, the Police put up with a lot of rowdiness and, at times, a fist fight or two. Naval Shore Patrols were also on duty in the area, and no doubt had many a tale to tell about the exploits of 'Jolly Jack' ashore.

My daily work station was in the ship's Confidential Books Office, working under one of the Royal Marine officers who was in charge of the confidential books and signal publications, CBs and SPs. New books and documents came aboard at times. This kept me busy entering amendments in the various books and publications held in the CB Office. We had to take great care in accounting for these books as the loss of one could have been exceedingly serious. I liked my job and got on with it.

For Action Stations, as I was a Corporal and a gunlayer, I was put in charge of one of the new quick firing 40-mm Bofors anti-aircraft quadruple mountings. Our action station was up in the port side after superstructure. This proved to be a good location, being in an open position we had an excellent view of the sea and other ships in company with us, but it was rather close to the four 14-inch guns of "Y" turret on the quarterdeck, and the after 5.25-inch turret.

HMS Duke of York sailed from Grand Harbour on the 25 May. The ship's company paraded on the upper deck for leaving harbour, each Division at its own part of ship. The Royal Marines were on the quarterdeck with the band. Formal salutes were exchanged with other ships and the signal station, as we slowly steamed past them. The salute took the form of a bugle call sounding 'The Still', followed by the dipping and raising of the White Ensign. The ship's company would be called to attention and ordered to face to Port or Starboard as the case may be. Once we had past the ship being saluted there would be another bugle call 'The Carry-on' and we would be ordered to stand at ease again. Upon passing the breakwater we were dismissed and took up our normal duties in the ship.

We had been at Malta for three weeks and it had been a busy time. On the messdecks some of the lads said they had had some good runs ashore in the evenings,

HMS Duke of York

and recounted their experiences in the bars, cafes and clubs in and around Strait Street, Valletta. The dghajsa men had had plenty of fares rowing the libertymen back to the ship at night.

We were soon brought back to the job ahead of us as we sailed past Mersa Matruh on the 27th on our way to Port Said. Our naval gunnery was exercised with a series of bombardment firings. The 14-inch guns go off with a fair old wallop, and in our open position we could feel the blast, but it was interesting for we could just catch a glimpse of the big shells disappearing into the distance as they sped towards their target.

The ship entered the Suez Canal and anchored for the night of the 28th in the Great Bitter Lakes. The powerful lights illuminating the gangway ladders during the night were shining on the surface of the water and attracting a host of different types of fish. This was not the place to have a swim I thought.

Next day we weighed anchor, past Port Tewfik and made our way into the Gulf of Suez. During our passage through the Suez Canal a tug held the bows of *HMS Duke of York* on a long tow rope to keep us in the correct part of the channel. There was not much free space between the ship's keel and the bottom of the canal. The weather was getting progressively hotter as we sailed south through the Red Sea. On the inshore side of us we occasionally saw Arab fishing boats. We passed Aden on the 2 June and headed for Colombo, Sri Lanki (Ceylon).

We entered Colombo harbour on the 8 June. The place was full of shipping; I saw a number of rusty old merchant ships tied up to harbour mooring buoys. In no time a small fleet of local traders' boats, bobbing about on the harbour water, came alongside with all sorts of wares, and started to do business over the ship's side. We were here for eight days and all the company had plenty of shore leave, and sightseeing tours. I missed out on a tour to Kandy, a religious shrine up in the mountains, more or less in the centre of the Island.

We left Colombo on the 16th and sailed for Sydney. Two days out from Colombo, during our crossing of the Indian Ocean, we were in the vicinity of the Equator, no doubt the first time for many of us onboard. Stories circulated the messdecks about the 'Crossing the Line' ceremony, and the dire deeds done to the first timers.

A typical ceremony would commence with an exchange of messages delivered by Flying Fish couriers, as follows:-

"To: H M Ship.
From: Equator Hydro Telegraphic Station.

The following message has been received from His Maritime Majesty King Neptune, by the Grace of Mythology, Lord of all Waters, and Sovereign of all Oceans.
(Begins) "My Southern Seas Patrol reports that H M Ship is proposing to enter my illustrious domain for the first time. Queen Amphitrite and I are much looking forward to your visit, and my Bears are delighted to hear of the large numbers of novices on board. We shall arrive on the forecastle with a fanfare of trumpets, roars of Bears, and members of my Court for the Ceremony of Initiation in accordance with the ancient custom of the Seas. Please make adequate preparations." (Ends)

To: Equator Hydro Telegraphic Station.
From: H M Ship.
Please pass to King Neptune.

(Begins) "We thank your Majesty for your gracious message. All those who have been initiated into the solemn rites of your Kingdom send their best wishes to you and your most Gracious Queen, All preparations are being made for the many novices to become true sons of your Realm in accordance with ancient custom." (Ends)

H M King Neptune then issued a Royal Proclamation constituting His Court from the ship's company as follows:-

Queen Amphitrite and two Mermaids, Dolphinius Chief Herald and Ambassador, two Trumpeters, a Judge, a Clerk of the Court, four Royal Doctors, eight Royal Barbers, a Court Jester, a Chief of Police, twenty-four Policemen, and thirty-five Royal Bears. No wonder King Neptune had a tough retinue. He needed them to round up over fifteen hundred novices, many of whom seemed to find a good reason for not wanting to be initiated.

At the appointed time, a lookout in a voice loud and clear reported, "Line ahead, Sir." Trumpets sounded as King Neptune, King of the Deep wearing his crown and carrying his trident appeared on deck with his Queen and retinue, all suitable dressed for the occasion, to be greeted by the Commander. The Royal procession formed up and made its way to the Quarterdeck, to be welcomed by our Captain.

King Neptune replied,

> *"Captain, Officers and crew,*
> *we're very glad to welcome you.*
> *We note with great and royal glee*
> *that many novices in the ship there be.*
> *My Bears are longing to get at 'em*
> *even if they're not from Chatham.*
>
> *Honoured we are that they cross our path*
> *and may they all enjoy the bath.*
> *My Bears, I know, will treat them rough;*
> *they're a hungry lot and very tough.*
> *And now to business. We've much to do*
> *before this Royal Court is through.*
>
> *Clerk of the Court, hand me the Orders*
> *for those who cross our Royal Borders."*

After a further exchange of dialogue by others members of the Court, The Chief Barber then reports:-

> *"Your Majesty's orders have been obeyed.*
> *The bath is overproof, the soap cream laid,*
> *the pills and tonic strong and undiluted,*
> *the razor keen, the water well polluted."*

King Neptune replies,

> *Now see that none do take offence.*
> *Let loose the Bears. Sound the 'Commence'".*

It was now time for us novices, officers and men, to be rounded up and taken before the Court on the upper deck. After the Clerk of the Court read the Warrant in true Naval slang the Judge pronounced:-

"*I do hereby adjudge him the aforesaid to be well and truly lathered, shaved and thrown to the Bears without delay, ducked twice until he bubbles.*"

Each initiate was unceremoniously placed in one of the chairs which were rigged over a canvas swimming pool full of sea water. Our faces were lathered with naval soap and a paint brush, shaved with an outsized wooden cut throat razor then tipped backwards, with arms and legs flying in the air, into the swimming pool. Matters did not end there. The Bears grabbed hold of us and we were ducked under the water several times, finally other helpers dragged us out of the pool, half drowned and gasping for breath. King Neptune had well and truly welcomed us to his domain. A few days later we received our Crossing the Line Certificates.

It was good fun, a well-deserved break in the ship's daily routine. In fact, an almost peace time feeling was in the air. But it felt strange, we were between two wars, one in Europe which had ended a few weeks ago, and the other still raging, many thousands of miles ahead of us.

As *HMS Duke of York* steamed on its way across the Indian Ocean towards Australia, flying fish scuttled away, skimming the surface of the waves as the hull of the ship disturbed them. Often lines of flotsam were to be seen in the sea, provoking thoughts of where did it come from, and what caused it?

After brief calls at Fremantle and Albany we sailed eastwards with the south coast of Australia to port.

As the ship neared the coast of New South Wales, we went on deck a number of times to look at the distant coastline. Announcements from the bridge kept us informed of our progress. On the messdecks there were plenty of discussions about Australia and Sydney, what a great place it was. Some of the lads said that they had heard that New Zealand was even better. However, we were all eager to get ashore in Sydney. There was near disbelief when the ship's company were warned that because of the Licencing Laws in Australia the bars stopped serving beer at 6 pm. The only places we had had shore leave since leaving the UK, 12000 miles and nine weeks away, were when we called at Malta and Colombo.

HMS Duke of York passed through the Heads of Sydney Harbour on the 1 July 1945, to a welcome by a host of small boats in the harbour, and people waving to us. It was quite an exciting time. We had paraded on the upper deck for entering harbour, and the band was playing. Eventually the ship anchored in the harbour near the Sydney Harbour Bridge.

On the 11th we had a visit from HRH The Duke of Gloucester, Governor General of Australia.

We were at Sydney until the end of the month. Dockyard workers got busy fitting additional close range anti aircraft weapons to the ship. We intensified our work up exercises at Jervis Bay, checking damage control and action stations procedures.

On the 31st we left Sydney and sailed north through the Coral Sea, and arrived on Sunday, the 5 August, at Manus, a British base in the Admiralty Islands near the equator. Next day, The Commander-in-Chief, British Pacific Fleet, Admiral Sir Bruce Fraser embarked with his staff, and hoisted his flag. *HMS Duke of York* then sailed as the Flag Ship British Pacific Fleet. Two destroyer escorts were assigned to us,

The officers and men of the United States Pacific Fleet and shore activities on Guam take pleasure in extending a hearty welcome to the officers and ships' companies of HMS DUKE OF YORK, HMS WHELP, and HMS WAGER.

It is our desire that your stay in Guam may afford the fullest opportunity for rest and recreation, and the facilities of the Island are at your disposal. It is our further hope that your visit will provide opportunities for friendly companionship between personnel of the two navies, so closely linked in the common cause.

C.W. Nimitz

Fleet Admiral, United States Navy
Commander in Chief, U. S. Pacific Fleet and
Pacific Ocean Area

9 August 1945

The 13,000 mile track of the battleship HMS *Duke of York* for the period 23 June 1945 to 9 October 1945. The voyage from Sydney to Tokyo alone was about 4,500 miles.

the *HMS Whelp* and *Wager* - old friends as far as I was concerned. Last June they had accompanied *HMS Jamaica* from Greenock to Spitzbergen and back to Scapa Flow. It was known on the messdecks that the First Lieutenant of the *Whelp* was a Prince.

When I was on watch at my cruising station on the Bofors, I was able to see the low lying coral Islands of the tropical seas as we passed them. We also watched our escorts as their slim bows sliced through the sea sending out a bow wave as we steamed along at about 18 knots. The Duke, as the ship was sometimes called, was big and heavy and had a gentle roll with a little pitching and tossing in an average sea, but the smaller destroyers had a much livelier movement as they rode the swell.

We arrived at 0900 hours on the 9th at Guam, in the Mariana Islands, the Advanced Headquarters of the United States Pacific Fleet. Next day a ceremony took place on our quarterdeck. Our C-in-C, Admiral Fraser, acting on behalf of King George VI, invested the American Commander, Fleet Admiral Nimitz with the Order of Knight Grand Cross of the Order of the Bath.

The Americans invited us to have a run ashore on Guam. So we soon experienced the generous hospitality of the US

Servicemen. We were in various small groups. My group was given a short guided tour of the coast road.

When we got back to the base area, a stage show was in progress. Thousands of American servicemen were watching a group of well-known Hollywood stars who had come out to the Pacific to entertain the boys. The stage seemed a long way in front of us as we stood at the back of the large audience. Then we were taken to the camp area and offered cans of beer. It was the first time I had ever seen, or drank canned beer, it went down a trea in the hot weather. As dusk came on it was back to our ship, we were due to sail in the morning.

At breakfast time on the messdeck there was a big buzz that an Atomic Bomb had been dropped on Japan, and that there might be a surrender. Someone said to the Hostilities Only lads, "Don't get too excited, they will not be sending you home just yet."

Hiroshima was bombed on the 6th, and Nagasaki three days later. Years later I learned that, when I was with the RM Detachment at the Quebec Conference, the Prime Minister's papers on the Atomic Bomb project, code name Tube Alloys, were among the documents we had been guarding so closely.

HMS Duke of York's departure was delayed. However, we sailed from Guam on Monday, the 13th, to operate with the massive American 3rd Fleet, South of Japan.

On the 17th, we found ourselves with a task group of the British Pacific Fleet. There was one of our sister ships, the battleship *HMS King George V,* which had played a leading role in operations here, and fifteen other Royal Navy ships in company, including aircraft carriers. At about breakfast time on the 19th a floating mine was sighted and destroyed clear of our stern quarter. We had come upon the occasional floating mine before.

On the evening of the 20th *HMS Duke of York* took up station, at a distance of about one mile, on the American battleship *USS Missouri*. Meteorological reports indicated bad weather, so the fleets then steamed around, dodging a typhoon which caused some ships in the vicinity a bit of trouble, even some structural damage, but we were alright in *HMS Duke of York*, although green seas swept over the bows a few times, the impacts sending a shudder right through the ship. Sometimes the trough between the waves or swell was such that, when I was on the upper deck watching our escorts, only the tops of the masts of the destroyers could be seen until they rose again in full view and rode the next wave, sometimes as much as forty feet.

On the 22nd we were witness to an extraordinary sight. One thousand American carrier-borne airplanes flew, in squadrons, quite low over the fleet. I stood on our forecastle, with the off duty watch, and just gazed skywards at the sight. The aircraft flew off in the direction of Japan.

The 23rd saw us in yet another formation. We were with the *USS Missouri* and fourteen American capital ships: battleships, aircraft carriers and cruisers, plus their escorting destroyers - a mighty fleet indeed.

There was one day during this busy period when aircraft were reported in trouble overhead and hands had been called to the guard rails to report positions if any came down in the sea. I was on the starboard side, aft of the 5.25-inch turrets and watched a single-engined plane approach us from the stern quarter. The pilot waggled the wings of his plane, slowly flew past us on the starboard side, set his plane down on the sea between us and our destroyer escort and climbed out of his cockpit. By this time our momentum had taken us past the aircraft which was beginning to settle in the sea. However, one of our escorts was already on its way and safely picked up the pilot.

Monday, the 27 August 1945, was quite a significant day for us. *HMS Duke of York* was one of a number of warships of the Allied Fleets which entered Japanese territorial waters and anchored in Sagami Wan, a large bay south of the entrance to Tokyo Bay. Earlier our Commander had addressed the ship's company explaining the move and said that our degree of readiness was about to be increased from defence stations to action stations.

Although the Japanese Government had accepted the Surrender terms, there was just a suspicion that some individual Japanese might make a last ditch attack on the ships as we entered Sagami Wan. Therefore, everyman was to be alert, personnel on the upperdeck action stations were to keep a sharp lookout for suspicious movements in the sea in case of an attempted suicide, human torpedo attack.

So, at 0800 hours, I was closed up at action stations with my gun's crew on our Bofors mounting. We had a clear view of the ships in company around us, all flying their Ensigns. High above us, on both our masts, two of the largest White Ensigns we had onboard - Battle Ensigns- were flying fully extended in the breeze. I felt quite a tingling sensation as we made our way into the sheltered waters and anchored. Mount Fujiama was visible in the distance. It was shortly after 1300 hours when we stood down, and there was relief all round that there were no incidents with the Japanese.

Nevertheless, the main part of the Allied Fleet was still at sea covering our movements.

Whilst we were in Sagami Wan, waiting to go into Tokyo Bay two British servicemen, ex-Prisoners of War were discovered by an American picketboat swimming towards the ships, Private E Campbell of the Royal Army Service Corps and Marine John Wynn. The Americans eventually brought both men to *HMS Duke of York* for repatriation to the UK. John Wynn was allocated to our mess for the time being. He was in fairly good condition, both in health and spirit. We treated him in a normal manner and left him to adjust to his new surroundings, and speak about his experiences as the mood took him. However, curiosity soon got the better of some of our messmates but John did not seem to mind answering their many questions. The main question seemed to be, "had he seen or heard anything of the atomic bomb", to which John replied, "No". (In fact Hiroshima was about four hundred miles south west of Tokyo Bay).

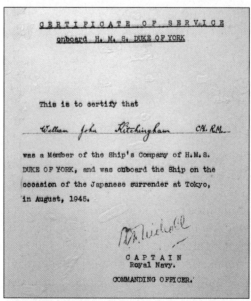

CERTIFICATE OF SERVICE
onboard H. M. S. DUKE OF YORK

This is to certify that

William John Kitchingham CH. RM.

was a Member of the Ship's Company of H.M.S. DUKE OF YORK, and was onboard the Ship on the occasion of the Japanese surrender at Tokyo, in August, 1945.

CAPTAIN
Royal Navy.
COMMANDING OFFICER.

There was still a tenseness in the air as we were called to action stations at 0845 hours on the 29th for a few hours whilst the flagships moved into Tokyo Bay itself. We anchored at 1145 hours, not far from *USS Missouri*.

HMS King George V sailed into Tokyo Bay at about noon the following day. And over the next two days many more ships arrived to swell the numbers in the anchorage.

The climax came on the 2 September 1945. The formal signing of the Surrender by Japan took place in the presence of General MacArthur and Allied representatives, onboard the *USS Missouri*, flagship of Admiral Halsey, Commander of the US 3rd Fleet.

At the time - it was not long after we had cleaned up the messdeck following breakfast - many of us on the *HMS Duke of York* were on the upper deck looking across the broad waters of Tokyo Bay at the *Missouri*, which was anchored not very far away from us. Our Commander-in Chief, Admiral Sir Bruce Fraser had gone, by Admiral's barge, to the *USS Missouri* to sign the Surrender document on behalf of the United Kingdom Government.

The war with Japan was over. Six years of war, bloody war had ended.

To mark the presence of *HMS Duke of York* in Tokyo Bay the staff of our General Information Office, who published the ship's newsheets, The Sunday Yorker and The Daily Yorker, produced a special six page V-J Day edition of 2000 copies. The last page was a Certificate to certify one's presence in Tokyo Bay on this historic occasion. The edition contained a special message from the Commander-in-Chief, Admiral Sir Bruce Fraser, to all the officers and men of the British Pacific Fleet, including those who served in the Fleet Train. There was also a message to our ship's company from our Captain, Captain A D Nicholl RN.

Many ships were now assigned to the repatriation of thousands of Allied servicemen from the Japanese prisoner of war camps all over the Far East.

HMS Duke of York left Tokyo Bay on the 9 September, and made a short call of a few hours at war torn Okinawa on the 11th, while on our way to Hong Kong. A number of Royal Navy ships were already in Hong Kong when we arrived on the 14th. We anchored in mid harbour with Kowloon on one side and Hong Kong Island on the other. Working parties were sent ashore to assist the civilian authorities as necessary. Armed patrols and escorts were still needed - Hong Kong was not yet safe for shore leave. In fact, from our upperdeck we could clearly hear short exchanges of small arms fire coming from the Hong Kong side of the harbour.

On the 16th Admiral Fraser went ashore to be present at the meeting at Government House when the Japanese formally surrendered Hong Hong to Rear Admiral Harcourt.

A day later I was sent ashore with another corporal and a section of armed marines to escort one of our naval officers to the Royal Navy's China Fleet Club premises, which were situated not far from the water front. Whilst the naval officer went about his task of examining the structural state of the building, we had a look around the former lower deck club. It was now just a shell, with some pock marks in the walls where bullets had struck and knocked out small portions of plaster and concrete. All the wooden doors and window frames had been torn out, and there was not a stick of furniture in the place. Nevertheless, the RN China Fleet Club was to be re-established, to be the pride of the Royal Navy's lowerdeck personnel.

The Japanese had erected a large structure in the form of an oriental archway which dominated the skyline. This monument, commemorating the Japanese capture of the colony, was so unacceptable to the citizens of Hong Kong that a call for it to be raised to the ground came to fruition a few months later.

One day a marine who had been ashore on escort duty came back onboard with some photographs which he had been given. The photographs showed a Japanese soldier, with a drawn sword, beheading some local inhabitants by the water front. The victims were in a kneeling position bound hand and foot. One photograph showed the victim's severed head falling forward after the sword had struck, and two fountains of blood spurting upwards from the neck of the torso. One of our sergeants, who had been on the messdeck and who had seen the photographs, left the mess. He returned shortly afterwards and said that the photographs had to be handed in to the Captain's Office.

HMS Duke of York left Hong Kong on the 21 September, with the Commander-in-Chief onboard, for Sydney calling at Manila on the way. However, in Manila Harbour there were hundreds of wrecks and after we dropped our anchor the ship swung onto an uncharted wreck, luckily doing no damage. We also had onboard, for the 4500 mile voyage to Australia, a few civilian passengers who had suffered during their imprisonment by the Japanese, in Stanley Prison on Hong Kong Island.

As we steamed south, *HMS Duke of York* passed through the Dampier Strait, that stretch of water between the islands of New Guinea and New Britain, into the Solomon Sea, through the Coral Sea again and on to Sydney, arriving on the 9 October. Our special passengers, who had had a peaceful two weeks voyage, were taken ashore with our best wishes for their future.

The ship was at Woollomooloo Docks, and the Captain now granted long leave to the ship's company, so I requested a few days. I had heard about the Blue Mountains and decided to spend my leave there. A train took me from Sydney out past Parramatta and up to Katoomba in the Blue Mountains. I stayed at the Hydro Majestic Hotel from the 19th to 24th October 1945. I still have the hotel bill for £2.17.6 Australian pounds. It was a pleasure to walk along the footpaths among the trees and take in the magnificent mountain views which were covered in a blue haze. It is said that the Blue Mountains get their name from this blue haze which is caused by sunlight shining on microscopic droplets of oil from the eucalyptus trees floating in the atmosphere. One day twelve of us hotel guests went on an organised mini coach trip some twenty miles further into the mountain area to the Jenolan

Receipt for my leave, October 1945

Quarterdeck working parties, under the barrels of the
14 inch guns of 'Y' Turret, preparing to secure the stern of *HMS
Duke of York* to the quayside at Hobart, Tasmania, November
1945. The gun muzzles hold medallions of the ship's crest - the
White Rose of York.

Caves, a large system of very old caves, caverns and passageways worn in the limestone deposits. On the way back to the hotel we made a stop at the Old Court House, Hartley, and our driver related stories about outlaws and runaways of the 1800s who roamed this mountain area. The leave ended too soon and it was back to the ship. Onboard there was a buzz that someone had taken such a liking to Sydney that he jumped ship, that is, he had stayed ashore not intending to rejoin the ship. His service documents would have been marked 'Run'.

We left Sydney on the 3 November and sailed south to Hobart, Tasmania, for a courtesy visit. Before leaving Tasmania the Captain took the ship into the calm waters of Norfolk Bay for a few days, where we held a ship's sailing and rowing regatta. It befell me to take charge of a RM crew of one of the ship's whalers in one of the rowing races. We got into the boat which was tied up at the boom and I gave some orders to start rowing to the start line, which took us round the stern of the ship. However, the Captain's face appeared through one of the open portholes of his quarters and, in a benevolent manner, expressed his opinion of our oarsmanship. Blushing, all I could say was, "Very good, Sir", and looked back at the faces of the marines who were staring at me, and grimaced. Not a good day.

We arrived back at Sydney on the 21st and tied up alongside the jetty. During the war, Sydney had been the main headquarters for the British naval operations in the Pacific theatre, and now the HQ was to be moved to Hong Kong. So, on the 1 December at 1035 hours *HMS Duke of York* cast off the securing lines to the jetty and sailed from Sydney with the HQ Staff of the British Pacific Fleet onboard for Hong Kong via Singapore. There was a bit of a sea running as we sailed west across the Great Australian Bight and the standing order to keep off the forecastle in bad weather was in force.

On the morning of the 6 December 1945, there was a tragic accident with one of the Oerlikon close range weapons, resulting in one of our naval ratings dying of the injuries he received. Then during the late afternoon the Captain ordered the ship's speed to be reduced, the colours to be flown at half-mast and a burial at sea service was held as the body was committed to the deep. On the messdeck we felt what rotten luck it was for this to befall a shipmate now that the war was over.

We anchored off Fremantle at 0625 hours on the 7th and waited for a senior naval officer to come aboard, sailing again at 1850 hours into the warm waters of the Indian Ocean. A few days later we visited Christmas Island in passing, and then on to Singapore, arriving on the 14th, two weeks sailing since leaving Sydney.

The anchorage, known as Singapore Roads, was surrounded by numerous small, low lying islands covered with lush vegetation. Here on the Equator in harbour, even with the normal fresh air ventilation fans running, it was hot onboard and we were glad to have the wind scoops in the portholes to catch the fresh air for the messdeck. A large number of ships, naval and merchant, were moored in The Roads.

It was while we were here that we heard that some servicemen had gone blind from drinking local booze which had been contaminated. This news put a quick end to Saki tasting.

The conferences between Admiral Lord Louis Mountbatten, Supreme Allied Commander, South East Asia and Admiral Sir Bruce Fraser, Commander-in-Chief British Pacific Fleet being completed we were on our way again. We sailed from Singapore on the 17th and headed north through the South China Sea on the four day trip to Hong Kong.

Two days out, with the south east coast of Vietnam over the horizon on our port side, we ran into squally weather. There appeared to be a problem with an anchor chain or something on the forecastle having worked loose and no longer properly secured, so the bridge 'piped' for a working party to muster behind the safety of the breakwater while the First Lieutenant went forward to investigate and decide what action was required. Suddenly a wave broke over the bows of the ship. Tons of green sea water fell on the First Lieutenant and washed him overboard on the port side. He was never seen again despite efforts to search for him. There was sadness onboard at the loss of an important member of the ship's company.

HMS Duke of York arrived back in Hong Kong on the 21 December 1945, anchoring in mid-harbour at about 1300 hours. Arrangements were then put in hand for us to relieve *Anson's* armed shore party, Kennedy Force.

At the beginning of September 1945, when Royal Navy ships entered Hong Kong harbour following the end of hostilities with Japan, the Captain of the battleship *Anson* put a strong force of armed marines and naval ratings ashore under the command of Commander A R Kennedy RN, to secure key areas and to maintain civil order. This detachment became known as Kennedy Force; it did a good job, and for his leadership Commander Kennedy received the Order of the British Empire Medal.

The day after we arrived back in Hong Kong I was detailed for shore patrol, with two marines, for duty in the Fleet Club and Wanchai area. Whilst ashore I came to an open-fronted woodworking shop, where three craftsmen were making large wooden chests and small boxes covered in oriental carvings. As a memento of being in Hong Kong, I asked for a cigarette box to be made with '*HMS Duke of York*' carved in the lid and 'Hong Kong 1945' on the back. When I returned a few days later to collect the box the workmen had added, as a nice gesture, 'Good Luck' and 'Long Life', in Chinese characters on the sides. I still have the box.

We spent Christmas, Tuesday 25 December 1945, onboard. The ship's company mustered for Divisions at 0915 hours, followed by Church Service on the quarterdeck. The remainder of the day was fairly quiet on the messdecks. Next day our marines and naval ratings went ashore to relieve Kennedy Force; *Anson* then sailed from Hong Kong. I volunteered for a spell with the Force but was told I was needed in the CB Office.

New Year's Day 1946 was celebrated by the RN ships in harbour giving an impressive fireworks display. Fireworks, of course, are one of the things in life that the Chinese enjoy.

On the 17 January, with Admiral Fraser onboard, we sailed north up the Chinese coast about 250 miles for a two day courtesy visit to Amoy. The ship's football team played a match against a Chinese team and won 8-1. The teams were presented to Admiral Fraser, and he and the Chinese Admiral started the game by kicking-off. The Royal Marine Band played before the game and during the half-time interval. Unfortunately, we did not see Amoy at its best. The weather was damp which gave the place a dreary atmosphere. Nevertheless we were pleased to meet the Chinese, and they us. *HMS Duke of York* arrived back in Hong Kong on the 21st.

Sightseeing tours to the New Territories were now being offered. One day a group of us went by train from Kowloon past Fan Ling to the railway bridge over the Sam Chun River at Lo Wu on the international border with China. It just so happened that we strolled across the bridge and wandered some distance over the open rolling countryside into a village inside the Chinese side of the border. But it soon transpired, from the attitude of the villagers, that we had ventured further than we should have. So it seemed prudent to make our way back to the railway bridge without delay. Nevertheless, two severe looking Chinese officials, dressed in khaki uniforms and riding horses, appeared on the edge of the village just as we got back to the border crossing.

March turned out to be a busy month. A number of ships arrived in Hong Kong, including one on the 7th with 45 Commando RM onboard, and it was not many hours before they took up security duties. The senior Commando officers paid a courtesy visit to the ship and the wardroom. Later they came below to the CB office and had a meeting with the CB Officer.

On the 10th, Admiral Fraser and his staff left the ship and moved into the shore headquarters.

Our members of Kennedy Force had now been relieved and returned onboard. But on the 11th they staged a very successful Tattoo ashore. Later that evening *HMS Duke of York* sailed out of Hong Kong, and headed north east for the Japanese island of Kyushu.

On the morning of the 15th we arrived in Nagasaki where the second atom bomb had exploded seven months earlier. I was in the sick bay with a high temperature and sore throat with tonsillitis, and was unable to go on the upper deck, or to take advantage of one of the short tours ashore which had been arranged.

The ship sailed later that evening, and next day anchored at Kagoshima. It was here that a boxing meeting was held between a team from the 1st Division United States Marine Corps and our ship's team. It was a very interesting meeting, seven fights were staged and it was not until the last fight that the US Marine Corps won the match by 4 fights to 3. Our team consisted of one midshipman, one able seaman and five Royal Marines.

Nearby, a small volcano was discharging a fine white ash which drifted on the wind, and the upperdeck looked as though it was covered in snow. However, upon sailing on the 18th we ran into a very heavy downpour, and the rain soon washed away the ash. In the meantime I left the sick bay and returned to duty.

The ship sailed on to the southern part of the island of Honshu and, after a very pretty trip through the Inland Sea, arrived at Kure on the 19th. Next day an amenity ship, an ex-Blue Funnel Line ship, the *Menestheus*, which had a small brewery, the 'Davy Jones' Brewery', installed, tied up on our starboard side for three days. Everyone had the opportunity of seeing a show, and having two sessions at the beer bars and cafeteria. A floating NAAFI manned by men of the Naval Canteen Service.

Sightseeing tours of this area of Japan, including visits to Hiroshima, were organised by the United States Authorities. A group of us from my mess decided to take advantage of this, and put our names down to form a party. We left the ship at 0825 hours, and a train took us the few miles from Kure to Hiroshima. Most of our party had first-hand experience of bomb and fire damage to our home towns and cities in the United Kingdom, but there was something different about the ruins of Hiroshima, it had been blasted and incinerated by one bomb, an Atomic Bomb. The main streets to which we were firmly restricted had now been cleared of debris so we were able to walk through the place. The gutted shells of the steel-reinforced concrete buildings, and a few other strongly built places, were still standing, of which the railway station was one. The remaining structures had been reduced to ashes. At one place I saw four dark green glass bottles, lying on the ground, welded together in a row.

We walked as far as a bridge and back to the station for the return trip to Kure, and were back onboard by 1430 hours.

Kure had also suffered greatly from repeated conventional bombing raids by the Americans. The Kure dockyard area, through which the train made its way, was a shambles. I saw the gutted hull of a large Japanese battleship lying in a dock.

Back onboard, on our mess at least, the general feeling and discussion was that the Atomic Bombs had to be used to force the Japanese to surrender, the argument being that, had assault landings been made on the Japanese home islands, the casualties on both sides would have been high. After all, we were serving onboard a battleship as part of a Task Force of the fleet which would have been committed, so we felt that many American and Allied servicemen's lives had been saved by the use of this weapon, and the war brought to an end much earlier than it might otherwise have been.

On the 24th the ship left Kure for Yokohama where we arrived on the 26th. Here about 1,200 of the ship's company went on a visit to Tokyo under the auspices of the American authorities. On our arrival in the Japanese capital we were formed into small groups and taken on a tour of the city. At one stop we saw the shrub lined walls and water filled moat behind which lay the palace of the Emperor of Japan.

Before returning to our ship we were entertained at an American servicemen's

HMS Duke of York riding at anchor at Kagoshima, Japan. A small volcano in the hills in the background is producing a discharge of volcano dust some of which settled on the ship's upperdeck, 17 March 1945.

centre, the Ernie Pyle Theatre, for coffee and doughnuts. And a stage show with Japanese artists ended the day in Tokyo.

HMS Duke of York sailed from Yokohama on the 27 March, and it was back to Sydney, arriving on the 10 April. The ship was then put into the Captain Cook Dock for maintenance. During our time in Sydney some former Marines, who had taken their discharge from the service at the end of the war to stay in Australia, came back onboard to say 'Hello' to the boys. They said they were doing well, some working in a cotton mill and some went to sea on fishing boats.

The HOs, Hostilities Only, ranks were being repatriated. We were losing good and sincere friends, but hoped to keep in touch with them through the Royal Marines Association.

On the 15 May 1946 it was time to say, 'Goodbye Sydney, we will always remember your warmth of welcome and kindness.' *HMS Duke of York* sailed out of Sydney Harbour with a fantastic flotilla of small boats and yachts escorting us to the Sydney Heads. When the ship got into the open sea she started a gentle roll from the effects of the long Pacific swell as we turned north for the two week voyage to Hong Kong.

In almost every ship of the Royal Navy there were enterprising men who, in their spare time, operated essential 'private firms'. On our Royal Marines Messdeck, of about three hundred ranks, we had a couple of marines who took on tailoring; sewing on new badges, repairing and altering uniforms. There were barbers, one was actually on my mess, and there was a boot and shoe repair 'firm'. Some men were very good at making toys.

In my off duty time I used my photograph tinting set to put some colour into the black and white photographs of my messmate's wives and girlfriends. I had already tinted a photograph of Patricia which they admired and wanted their's done. When we were in Japan I obtained a black and white photograph of Mount Fujiama and tinted it. In fact I still have the photograph and it looks quite good.

When the ship was at sea, weather conditions permitting, deck hockey which was a popular recreation was held in the late afternoons on the upperdeck. A series of Knock-out Competitions were organized and in the second series forty five teams from all the divisions of the ship's company took part. The matches were rough and tough with quite a lot of body contact. In any one game up to six pucks could be knocked overboard, so a rating was on the side lines with a sack of pucks, made from off-cuts of wood, ready to throw replacements into the game.

A couple of seamen indulged in weight lifting and wrestling. A small crowd could often be seen watching them working-out. However, if these activities were too strenuous there was always the popular 'Egyptian PT' which had a large number of devotees; it consisted of finding a quiet spot and having a snooze.

We entered Hong Kong harbour on the 29th May. A 'Buzz' had been going round the messdecks that we were going home shortly.

On the 7 June Admiral Lord Fraser came onboard, and we finally sailed out of

Hong Kong to begin our five week journey home to the United Kingdom. We made a short call at Singapore on the 11 June, then on to Colombo for three days. We sailed on the 18th for the longest leg of our journey home, nine days at sea, across the Arabian Sea, passed Aden into the Red Sea and up to the Suez Canal.

HMS Duke of York passed Port Tewfik and anchored in the Great Bitter Lake on the 27th, here the Captain gave permission for hands to swim, but I did not fancy it. I remembered seeing the weird fish here when we were on our way to the Pacific last year.

The weather during our passage through the Suez Canal was fairly cool, which was a great relief to all onboard. Especially for the boiler room and engine-room watchkeepers, who had put up with some very trying conditions during our time in the tropics. The great ship gently touched the bottom of the canal four times as we slowly made our way to Port Said at the north end of the canal.

The Royal Navy aircraft carrier *HMS Indefatigable* passed us in Port Said, with a smart detachment of W.R.N.S. lining the after end of the flight deck. A great cheer went up from our hands on the upperdeck at such a spectacle.

On the 30th, as *HMS Duke of York* left Port Said we fired a 21-gun salute to the country of Egypt. The Egyptian shore batteries courteously returned the salute.

During our passage through the eastern part of Mediterranean Sea, from Port Said to Malta, the Captain stopped the ship a couple of times for 'Hands to Bathe' over the side. Ship's boats were lowered into the sea as safety patrols for the swimming area. I enjoyed it very much, and had not given much thought to the fact that the sea bed was a long way below us.

We stopped in Grand Harbour, Malta from the 3 to 5 July, and then sailed on to Gibraltar, arriving on the 8th. Here liberty men had a few hours ashore and brought a load of bananas onboard to take home.

The day we had all been looking forward to arrived as, on the 11 July 1946, *HMS Duke of York* sailed into Plymouth Sound. We were all lined up on the upperdeck for entering harbour and the band was playing lively tunes. Looking ashore we could see crowds of people on vantage points along the Hamoaze waving to us. It was a lovely summer's day, a joyous occasion, as the ship made its way up river. We tied-up alongside the jetty at the Royal Naval Base, Devonport, and it was great to see our wives, families and friends crowding the quayside. Our Captain welcomed them on the forecastle as soon as the gangways were in position, and invited them to stay for supper on the messdecks.

It was the first time the ship had been in her home port. Soon afterwards many of the detachment were in Stonehouse Barranks and able to enjoy their end-of-war leave before their next posting.

A few weeks later the ship's company was further reduced in numbers while the ship underwent a short refit period. We had to stay onboard as one of the Corporals of the Gangway, working in watches. Then on the 26 November 1946 the crews of *HMS Duke of York* and *HMS King George V* swapped ships. *HMS Duke of York* was to take over as Flag ship, Commander-in-Chief Home Fleet.

I was now a Corporal of the Gangway onboard *HMS King George V* which was tied up to buoys in the river off Devonport. She was paid off in December but I had to stay onboard and did not return to Stonehouse Barracks until the 17 January 1947.

Here are a few facts and figures on the *HMS Duke of York* during her second commission; from April 1945 to July 1946: steam on main engines for 222 days out of 476, steamed 58,413 miles, used 50,744 tons of fuel oil; 58,086 tons of drinking water had been consumed of which 26,086 tons were distilled onboard in addition 25,840 tons of distilled water made for the boilers.

Chapter 8
42 Commando RM, Hong Kong and Malaya

During the rather cold winter months of 1948-49 I was with a group of sergeants on a Commando conversion course at the Commando School, Royal Marines, Bickleigh, Devon, and on completion we exchanged our blue berets with the red patch for the Commando green beret.

On the 24th March 1949, I was drafted to 42 Commando RM in Malta, and assigned to 'Y' Troop as a section sergeant. Overseas duty in these times was usually for two years and six months. 42 Commando RM, at this time, consisted of about 600 officers and men; organised into four Rifle Troops, 'A', 'B', 'X', and 'Y', a Support Weapons Troop and a Headquarters Troop.

Within a few weeks of my arrival the Unit went to Waterfall Camp at Tarhuna, which lies in the desert about fifty-five miles south of Tripoli, for a period of desert warfare training. We were transported with all our fighting equipment and vehicles in Royal Navy vessels known as Landing Ships Tank - LSTs - from Malta to Tripoli Harbour. The beach, where the LSTs moored and lowered their ramps for the road transport to disembark, was littered with bits and pieces of old and useless small arms ammunition. And on the road journey into the desert we came upon the occasional stack of World War Two artillery shells by the side of the road.

At Waterfall Camp the Commando was allocated troop bivouac areas, shaded from the sun by a number of trees and shrubs. Bivouacking was an activity the experienced marine had developed to a fine art. Here we would dig down into the hard packed sand as though digging a slit trench, cover it with a two man tent and live in it during our six week stay. However, in Malaya a vastly different technique of bivouacking had to be employed, there we constructed "bashas" basically using our poncho waterproof capes. I remembered an old marine in Stonehouse Barracks telling me once that, with a little ingenuity, soldiering need not be too uncomfortable. Nevertheless, whether we were in the desert or in the jungle, each environment had its problems to be dealt with, such as dust storms and scorpions in the desert, or rain and leeches in the jungle.

Waterfall Camp was located by a small stream which tumbled over a rocky outcrop in the sand. A small pool had been blasted out of the rocky river bed at the base of the waterfall by our assault engineers, to make a pool suitable for splashinq about in after our military exercises in the sandy training areas.

Once during a rest period I went with a small group of senior non-commissioned officers to the ruins of the ancient Roman City of LEPTIS MAGNA, situated on the North African coast by the Mediterranean Sea. For many centuries the site had been covered in sand dunes which had now been cleared away to reveal these marvellous ruins. We walked the streets, and looking down saw the wheel ruts worn in the street paving slabs. I took the opportunity to sit in one of the back rows of seats in the large, well preserved amphitheatre and, looking down at the stage area, let my mind contemplate the activity here over 1,700 years ago.

The Unit arrived back in Malta on the 8 June and moved into St Patrick's Barracks. In our off duty hours, as the weather was now fine, we went swimming daily in the nearby clear sea.

In no time at all we were told to get ready for a move to Hong Kong, embarking in the former troopship Georgic on the 21st July 1949. On passing through the Suez Canal, during the period 25th and 26th, we embarked 45 Commando RM. The whole 3rd Commando Brigade, 40, 42 and 45 Commandos RM together with Brigade Headquarters and the Brigade Band, was now onboard. This was a comfortable trip. Georgic had been taken off trooping and was fitted out with cabins for the immigrant runs from the United Kingdom to Australia, but on this occasion the ship was used to transport us to Hong Kong.

During the passage suitable training sessions were arranged such as small arms training including live firings over the ship's stern. There were also a number of lectures on the history, political and military situation in China and Hong Kong. Checks were made to ensure that we were up-to-date with our vaccinations and inoculations against the various diseases in this part of the world. Our unit doctor gave talks on keeping well in a tropical climate, and on the types of snakes in the area. Inter-Commando sports helped pass the time, and there was a good library onboard so we were able to do quite a lot of reading in our cabins.

Georgic called at Aden on the 29th July, Singapore on the 8th August, and entered Hong Kong waters on the 13th August 1949, a little over three weeks sailing from Malta. So I was back in Hong Kong again. It was on the 7th June 1946 when I sailed away in *HMS Duke of York*.

The whole Brigade disembarked at Kowloon Docks, on the New Territories side of the harbour. Military bands played as we came down the gangways, and a soft drinks company was handing out bottles of orangeade from stacks of crates on the quayside. It was most welcome as the weather was hot and sticky, but a bottle of ice cool beer would have gone down a treat. Nevertheless, this particular brand of soft drink became a favourite with us.

While 40 and 45 Commandos were deployed in other areas of the Colony, 42 Commando RM set up camp at Chatham Road, on level ground beside the railway line leading into Kowloon Station. The trains from China were so crowded that people were sitting on the roofs, and hanging onto the sides of the coaches.

We were under canvas, and had duckboards inside the tents to keep our beds and

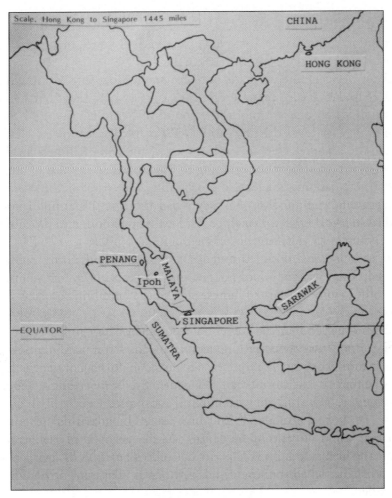

Scale. Hong Kong to Singapore 1445 miles

CHINA

HONG KONG

PENANG

Ipoh

MALAYA

SARAWAK

SINGAPORE

SUMATRA

EQUATOR

42 Commando Royal Marines
Hong Kong and Malaya

kit off the ground which soon got wet in the heavy rains. Each member of the unit was issued with a lockable "Soldier's Box" - a locally made wooden box about as large as a medium sized suitcase - in which to stow items of kit and personal belongings.

The chorus of hundreds of croaking frogs in the camp at night had to be heard to be believed, they were even under the duckboards inside the tents. Three weeks later, on the 7th September 1949, a typhoon struck the general area of Hong Kong and totally wrecked our camp. Sheets of corrugated iron flying on the very strong winds were a most dangerous hazard.

A temporary move was made into nearby Whitfield Barracks while the typhoon blew itself out. We then reestablished our camp, sorting and drying out our kit and equipment. A permanent move into Whitfield Barracks was completed on the 21st September 1949.

During the typhoon something hit me on my left knee causing quite a gash. Within hours my knee had become infected and swollen, so our unit doctor sent me into a casualty reception centre where I was kept for about 48 hours, being given penicillin injections which soon cleared up my injury.

A couple of weeks before we made our permanent move into Whitfield Barracks, I noticed a civilian marquee being erected on a grassy patch just outside our camp perimeter fence. Then one afternoon the sound of hymn singing and the strident voice of an evangelist came drifting our way. Next day I went to see what it was all about. Inside the marquee were a few Europeans, and some Chinese in their white shirts, sitting on rows of benches listening to the enthusiastic voice of an American preacher who was standing at a lectern proclaiming with passion, the salvation of the human race through his mission. All very well I thought, a real hot gospeler, but I felt he had a long way to go to convince the local population who probably thought Buddhism, Taoism or Confucius had some merit.

The war with Japan had ended four years ago and Hong Kong was recovering from its ordeal. There was civil war in China and elements of the Army of the People's Republic began to appear on the Chinese side of the border in the New Territories, and it looked fairly certain that the Chinese National Army, under Generalissimo Chang Kai-Shek would soon no longer have power in China.

Training started shortly after our arrival in Kowloon, and then we became operational for internal security duties. 42 Commando RM was also engaged in a number of small patrols to outlying villages in the New Territories and helping, where possible, any sick villagers with medical assistance.

'Y' Troop developed into a well-knit unit under Lieutenant Anthony Stoddart RM, who was acting Troop Commander. Each member of the Troop pulled his weight and there was a good rapport between all ranks. As a Troop we had a couple of weeks in a small training camp in the lush vegetation at Sai Kung, in the New Territories.

A Brigade Rifle Shooting Competition had been organised at the Royal Marines Training Unit on Stonecutters Island just before Christmas 1949. Teams from 40, 42 and 45 Commandos RM took part, and there was good rivalry between the teams, but 42 Commando as a team came last, although there were some individual successes.

Various large scale military exercises were taking place. I remember one exercise which entailed walking up hundreds of steps, in the dark, carrying heavy loads on our backs and deploying along a defence line on the high ground overlooking Kai Tak, Hong Kong's airport.

Half way up, the Brigade Commander, Brigadier C R Hardy came climbing up the steps behind our troop with his pack on his back and, in a light hearted manner, inquired how we were making out, well knowing that it was 'quite a puff' and a strain on one's legs. There was some good humoured banter from the lads, such as, 'who dreamt this up?' The Brigadier smiled and went on past. The exercise ended after about thirty six hours and we went back to Whitfield Barracks.

In barracks my room, or as we would say cabin, was on the ground floor at the end of one of the accommodation blocks. One day someone stole my civilian clothes.

I told our unit Provost Sergeant about this and he said that, as we had a number of Chinese workers in the barracks, he would have to inform the Hong Kong Police. I was astounded when my sports coat and flannel trousers were returned to me a few days later.

Another incident was one night, when I was asleep in my cabin, someone slipped a sheet of burning newspaper through the slats of the window of my room onto my bed. Fortunately, the burning paper fell onto the concrete floor and harmlessly burnt out. The first I knew of this was when I awoke next morning, and saw the ash on the floor. I was unable to find out the reason for this incident.

Christmas 1949 was spent in Barracks with the usual tradition of the officers and senior non-commissioned officers serving Christmas dinner to the troops. The cooks had worked very hard in this climate to produce all the usual Christmas fare which was much appreciated by all ranks. The festive season in Hong Kong went very well.

In March 1950 I was given temporary promotion to Colour Sergeant and became a Troop Quartermaster Sergeant. A TQMS is usually a senior non-commissioned officer, responsible to the Troop Commander for the military stores of the troop and, when out in the field or on troop location, the rations and feeding of the troop personnel. A TQMS is usually a very resourceful and artful scrounger to the benefit of his troop.

The internal security duties of the 3rd Commando Brigade RM lessened as the months went by, tension in the area had eased. The industrious Hong Kong Chinese went about their commercial activities, building and developing the area. Merchant ships and large junks were discharging and loading cargo, and ferries and sampans were endlessly moving about the harbour. The Colony as a whole was a hive of industry.

Then, on the 3rd May 1950, the Brigade received a warning order to move to Malaya which was facing internal unrest. Advance parties were immediately dispatched to make the many necessary arrangements for our arrival, first on the small island of Penang, which lies just off the west coast of Malaya, and then in the State of Perak. The jungles of Malaya were about 1400 miles south of Hong Kong.

40 Commando RM, the first unit to move, was embarked in my old ship *HMS Jamaica* and left Hong Kong on the 23rd, disembarking on the 27th at Penang, before proceeding to the mainland. 45 Commando RM followed in the troopship *Empire Trooper* in early June, and 42 Commando RM embarked in the troopship *Devonshire* during the afternoon of the 10 June and sailed that night.

So, after ten months, I was saying goodbye to Hong Kong yet again. I had grown to like the place, and the people. It was goodbye to the 'Good Luck' Chinese vermilion paint that was somewhere on just about every building. It was goodbye to the 'Dragon'; the smell of camphor wood and joss sticks; the noise of firecrackers, Chinese music and, of course, the Hong Kong Harbour Ferries.

We called at Singapore on the 15th for a few hours, and then sailed on to Penang, arriving on the 16th. Accommodation had been prepared for the unit, with the Army, in Glugor Barracks. There were detailed briefings for all ranks on the Emergency facing Malaya. Lectures were also given on the commerce and industry of the area, and on the customs of the people. All ranks now had to undergo a period of jungle training. A change of uniform was necessary, our khaki drill being replaced with olive green clothing, which had to be treated with an anti Scrub Typhus chemical. Jungle equipment was issued which included comfortable jungle boots, the universal jungle hat and a sharp machete. The usual medical advice was restated with firmness, to continue taking the anti-malaria tablets and to sleep under mosquito nets at night in camp. Insect repellent and small nets would be issued for patrol work as necessary. And not to forget the salt tablets.

Advice was also given on the recognition of dangerous wild life. A snake we had to be particularly wary of was the yellow banded krait, and instructions were given on first-aid for snake bite.

During a rest period I had a look around Georgetown, the main town in Penang, and also visited the Snake Temple. I was not all that keen, despite the temple attendant's assurances, on being surrounded by these reptiles, even though they were drowsy during the day, and coiled safely around the branches of tree stumps provided for them in the temple.

Towards the end of June news came through that war had broken out in Korea. The unit was busy with its preparations for the move to Ipoh, the principle town and commercial centre of the State of Perak - but orders could be changed. However, 40 and 45 Commandos RM had previously moved to the mainland, and were already in their new locations.

For the past few months I had been the Troop Quartermaster Sergeant of Headquarters Troop, and now, as we were about to leave Penang for Ipoh, I was required to take over as HQ Troop Sergeant Major. A Troop Sergeant Major, TSM, is the senior noncommissioned officer of the troop and is the Troop Commander's right hand man, responsible to him for the administration and discipline of the troop. I found this a very interesting appointment, working with the various sections of HQ.

Headquarters Troop moved on the morning of the 14th July 1950. We were ferried across the narrow straits, from Penang Island to the Malayan mainland and the railway station at Prai. Before personnel entrained, orders were issued on what action was required in the event of a bandit attack on the train, or if the line had been damaged and the train forced to stop. However, a pilot train would precede us. As we had a few minutes before departure, I went forward and had a look. It consisted of a small steam engine, with fortified flat top wagons ahead and behind it, manned by locally enlisted personnel armed with machine guns and rifles.

We left Prai Station for the seventy mile journey to Ipoh in carriages with hard seats. The railway track wound its way south across open country, over bridges and often through secondary jungle. Here the vegetation had been cleared back about ten yards on each side of the rails. We did not seem to be going very fast, probably about 20 or 30 miles per hour for short spells, and stopped a number of times which brought everyone to the alert but there were no incidents. As the afternoon drew on we ate our bag rations – sandwiches - which had been prepared for us by the cooks at Glugor Barracks.

The train arrived at Ipoh at 1715 hours, about five hours after leaving Prai, then road transport took us the short distance to Ashby Camp, on the outskirts of town. The base camp was quite large in area, low lying on open ground between the town and the scrubby edge of some secondary jungle - secondary jungle is basically vegetation that has grown where primary jungle has been cleared, and can be quite thick.

There was plenty of space for the Officers' Mess, Sergeants' Mess, Commando HQ offices, Brigade HQ offices, quartermaster's stores, a vehicle repair unit and a NAAFI - Navy, Army and Air Force Institution canteen for the Corporals and Marines. Some of the buildings were brick built. Others were made of wood, raised off the ground on short supports, and covered in attap, a local traditional covering material made from large leaves.

Our marines were accommodated, four men to a tent, in quite nice tents known as EPIPs (European Personnel, Indian Pattern) well able to stand up to the tropical climate. Tall plants with colourful flowers, which attracted a range of beautiful, large butterflies, grew in the ground around the tents and messes.

I was sharing a large airy room in the Sergeants' Mess block with the unit Physical Training Instructor. The whole area was hot and humid, and large overhead electric fans constantly stirred the air inside the rooms. For comfort, when off duty in the afternoons around our accommodation, but not in the mess, we wore colourful Malay sarongs around our waist, and flip flops on our feet.

Often in the late afternoons, while seated on the mess verandah in the shade of the overhanging roof, drinking tea and wiping away the perspiration on a towel, we would watch the almost daily thunder storm rumbling around the local hills. There were great flashes of lightning and claps of thunder accompanied with bursts of heavy rain.

When the rains came our way numerous deep monsoon ditches, which had been dug on each side of the roads, around the huts and tents, efficiently drained away these tropical downpours. The concrete lined monsoon ditches, however, presented a hazard to the unwary at night. We had two people fall into them resulting in head injuries.

The four fighting troops and support troop were deployed in troop locations around Ipoh, some as much as twenty-five miles away. They soon started patrolling their areas as it was very important to know the ground over which the bandits operated. Cooks, drivers and signallers were allocated to troop locations from HQ Troop.

It was now August 1950, and Korea had crept back into our conversation. The question was, would we be sent, would units from the UK be drafted out to relieve us, or would a unit go straight to Korea from the UK? One morning orders were received for the unit to come to one hour's notice to move. We got ready in our fighting equipment and were arranged into groups to go to the local airfield. However, by tea time we were stood down and returned to our former duties. Information came through that 41 (Independent) Commando RM had been formed in the UK and would be flown to Japan to operate as part of the United Nations effort in Korea.

One day in October 1950, I was one of a number of 42 Commando RM Officers and Senior Non-Commissioned Officers who were invited by the local Ghurkha Unit, which was stationed close by, to be their guests at Dashera, the principle Ghurkha festival. A few days earlier I had noticed a small area of ground, about thirty feet wide and fifty feet long, being fenced off a few hundred yards away from our HQ Office huts. A reminder had been issued to the Royal Marines that the Ghurkha festival of Dashera, which would last four days, was about to commence and that all ranks should be careful of their conduct. Rum, which is a favoured drink of the Ghurkhas, sustained the singing and dancing during their celebrations.

Senior Officers and important guests were seated in the front rows, and we took our seats in the back rows of the stand to witness the climax of this celebration. In the arena the Ghurkha Battalion's rifles were neatly piled in rows. At one end of the arena, to our right from where we sat, a sturdy post had been very securely placed in the ground. A hole had been bored through the post about twelve inches above ground level, and the area was decorated in Ghurkha fashion.

A few goats were led into the arena from our left, and while each animal, in turn, was held steady by two men a third Ghurkha, armed with a kukri, decapitated the goat with a single blow of his weapon. Another man took hold of the heads and poured water into the mouths, and laid the heads on the ground. The bodies were then dragged around the arena in a clockwise direction, leaving trails of blood on the ground, before being taken away. The meat was used later by the Ghurkhas for a feast.

A young male buffalo was then led in and placed before the decorated post. A rope was placed about its head and the end of the rope threaded through the hole in the post.

It was considered a great honour among Ghurkhas to be selected as the man to sacrifice the buffalo with a single blow, and thereby bring good luck to the unit for the ensuing year. The man, armed with an extremely sharp, oversized sacrificial kukri, placed himself to the left of the animal. The rope was tightened drawing the buffalo's head downwards. After checking the position of the vertebra on the beast's neck, the man raised the gleaming weapon high above his head and struck with all the force in his body. The blow made an ugly sound as the head was severed from the body and blood spurted out of the neck. A cheer went up from the Ghurkhas present, the act was indeed one blow, and good luck ensured. The body was also dragged around the arena, increasing the blood stains on the ground.

The 'sacrificer' then presented himself before the presiding officer who congratulated the man and tied the coveted white scarf of honour around the man's head, thus greatly enhancing the man's reputation in the battalion.

Back in our own Sergeants' Mess, over a cup of tea, we had quite a discussion on the prowess of Johnny Ghurkha and his kukri, the traditional, broad bladed, curved knife of these warriors.

It was nearing Christmas 1950, when our Regimental Sergeant Major said to me that he had the Commanding Officer's permission to lay on a social evening in the NAAFI for the Commando, and would I arrange it. This came as a surprise to me, however, I said that I would, and co-opted the Unit Physical Training Instructor and two other sergeants. We had a meeting and got on with the arrangements. The Brigade Bandmaster said that he would provide musicians to form a dance band and some instrumental solos. Volunteers from the sergeants and corporals came forward to do a turn or two - the 'One Armed Fiddler' and 'This old Shirt of Mine' went down a treat. A call went out around Ipoh inviting girls, and nurses from the local hospital to come and dance with the marines. The NAAFI Manager was quite happy with the arrangements, and closing time was extended. In case there should be any drink inspired trouble I laid on a few extra marines for picket duty, but there were no serious incidents.

On the night things were going with a swing, and well into the evening some of our officers arrived and joined in the fun. Then the Brigade Commander arrived. A cheer went up when he was recognised, and a wave of marines lifted him on to a table top to a spontaneous rendering of 'For He's a Jolly Good Fellow.' A respectful silence fell over the assembly as the Brigadier thanked the men for their greeting. He then got down from the table and circulated among the ranks.

After a few months as HQ Troop Sergeant Major I was appointed to relieve the Troop Sergeant Major of 'B' Troop. He had completed his tour of duty and was leaving the unit for home. But it was a sad time to join the Troop. A Marine had been killed a few days earlier when the Troop was out on patrol. The leading section was ambushed by a group of bandits who fired a few shots and ran off.

'B' Troop was located at the neat, clean, small township of Batu Gajah, about ten miles south of Ipoh. The camp was just off Siputhi Road at a Government Rest House, which was used as the Officers Mess. Other nearby buildings were used as the Sergeants Mess, the troop office and troop store. Service marquees accommodated the marines and army ranks.

As the Troop Sergeant Major, it was part of my duty to ensure that we had an efficient camp routine, including guards and sentries for the safety of our camp. It was particularly important that, under these tropical conditions, we should maintain as strict a camp hygiene as possible, enforced when necessary through the troop sergeants. An airy cookhouse had been constructed and the cooks, much to their credit, served a high standard of food.

We had in camp about eighty-five persons. Officers, SNCOs and men, including attached ranks, such as drivers, cooks and signallers, from HQ Troop. The number also included a section of Royal Army Service Corps drivers under their SNCO, Sergeant McGibbon. In marines terms he was known as, 'a good hand.'

We also had two Ibans from Sarawak, North Borneo, on short periods of service and at one time we had three of them. In camp they were allocated a tent in a quiet corner for their use. They had to look after themselves including their own cooking, which caused quite a smell at times. These jungle-wise men had dark skin heavily tattooed in traditional designs, sported straight black hair and had dangling ear lobes. When the military activities required it the Ibans, dressed in service jungle green uniform, helped us to track the bandits in difficult country.

Entrance to 'B' Troop 42 Commando RM Camp, Batu Gajah, 1951

In camp we had a few troop pets. A small monkey was kept in check with a light chain, but it was noisy and dirty. One day it disappeared, I am pretty sure none of us regretted it going. Every now and again, in the late afternoons, a troop of monkeys would emerge from the jungle and visit a group of tall trees growing about one hundred yards from our camp. They made quite a noise with their chatter, and the tree tops swayed as they jumped about in the branches. Then, just before darkness fell, which came quickly there being no evening twilight in the tropics, the monkeys moved off into the thickets.

Another pet which attracted the attention of visitors was a caged miner bird, with its calls and whistles.

Stray dogs found their way into camp. Unfortunately we could not keep them all and they had to be put down. However, two dogs were allowed. One named Toby used to greet the patrols as they returned to camp. He seemed pleased to see the marines and would follow them to their tents. The other dog acted as camp watchdog, raising the alarm if anything out of the ordinary occurred. One day I found him barking at a small snake which was making its way along the ground by the bamboo hedge. He would also visit the guard room, and accompany the camp wandering patrol on its rounds at night.

Geckos, small lizards, would come out at night and creep about on the ledges, walls and even on the ceilings of buildings preying on insects. In the Sergeants' Mess we were quite happy to let them run freely. Sometimes they would fall onto the wooden flooring with a plop, a sound we soon got used to.

Batu Gajah was where I developed the taste for a fine curry. The staff at the Government Rest House were mainly local Malays, polite friendly people, and when operations permitted, the Rest House cook would display his skill by cooking a really delicious Malayan curry with all the fresh fruit and vegetable side dishes. On occasions our Troop Commander would invite the members of the Sergeants' Mess to join him and the Troop Subalterns for a relaxing Sunday tiffin.

The country around Batu Gajah was flat, with swamps, streams and a river - a Sungei. The main west coast railway line ran through the town, and there were good main roads. A network of vehicle tracks ran through the district linking up villages, squatter shack areas, rubber plantations and the tin dredging sites. These areas were also served by a number of footpaths well worn by the natives. The local folk made great use of their bicycles, riding along the footpaths, tracks and even deep in the rubber plantations when working on the rubber trees, tapping the latex.

We made good friends with some UK engineers who worked on the tin dredgers in the jungle. These giant machines, floating in lagoons, manoeuvred themselves about with powerful winches pulling on long strong steel hawsers firmly anchored in the ground many yards away in the jungle.

The noise of the machinery was unmistakable as it clanked away, twenty-four hours a day, floodlit at night. An endless chain of large dredging buckets gouged out the water soaked aggregates. The heavy, valuable, fine black tin ore being extracted and the waste spewed out on long chutes onto the banks, scarring the jungle with tin tailings - expanses of barren sandy soil, which caused a glare in the sunlight.

42 Commando RM was responsible for the military operations in this part of the State of Perak, with 'B' Troop covering the Batu Gajah area. The bandits, organised in small groups terrorised the squatters, villagers, rubber and tin workers extorting from them food, money and information. They were callous and often murdered innocent people in their effort to keep a grip over the local population. They were elusive, using the tracks and footpaths with local knowledge, to quickly move about and disappear into their jungle hideouts.

It was a sad fact, however, that amongst the bands of terrorists who were murdering local people, and shooting at the security forces, were a small number of females. The bandits wore a green uniform and a cap with a red star on the front. They had packs on their backs and carried weapons. Being dressed alike it was not obvious who were females and three of them lost their lives when engaging 'B' Troop patrols.

We were well aware of the results, in human terms, of the sudden bursts of violence

Sergeant Wilson's patrol just returned to camp, Batu Gajah, 1951

from small arms fire at close range. The bodies of dead bandits were recovered by the sections involved, brought back to camp and then taken to the town mortuary for the Police and Civil Authorities to deal with.

Our operations were carried out with a mixture of patrols by sections of up to ten men led by a Sergeant, half troop patrols led by one of our Lieutenants and full troop operations under the Troop Commander. Sometimes the operation would take only a few hours, others a day or two. Not only were we sending out patrols against the bandits, with a good degree of success, but we were also involved with other co ordinated activities.

The Malayan Government was pursuing a national policy of resettling the small isolated squatter communities, upon which the bandits preyed, into defended settlement areas which helped to cut off the bandits' contact with the squatters. The RASC drivers and their vehicles, on detachment to our camp, were engaged in moving the families and their possessions into the new community areas in this part of Perak. When the move was in the Batu Gajah area, a patrol of 'B' Troop would provide protection against any interference from the bandits, and assist the people as necessary. This resettlement programme was going on throughout Malaya.

One afternoon, towards the end of January 1951, the local Civilian Authorities made a request to our Troop Commander for assistance in rescuing some Malay families who had been cut off by floods. There had been heavy rains up country and the rivers near Batu Gajah had risen and were flooding the low lying areas.

The Troop was committed to operational patrols, however, there were a few marines from the off-duty section in camp; so I said that I would get a group of volunteers together to help where we could. We quickly got dressed in our jungle green uniforms, and carried hand guns for protection, leaving rifles and machine guns in the troop store, we needed to travel light. A civilian liaison officer and a guide soon arrived in camp, and off we went in a Jeep and a two-ton truck which was fitted with a winch. A winching capability was essential in this type of country for pulling out a bogged down vehicle. About twenty minutes' drive from camp along a tarmac road we turned down a narrow dirt track overhung with trees, which cut down the sunlight, and stopped in a clearing. We could see the muddy flood water ahead, so we would have to wade about three hundred yards to the family's hut set among the trees. The water was up to my hips by the time we got to the stranded families. Daylight was just beginning to fade, and if we did not get a move on keeping direction on the way back would be a problem.

I had a child, about three years old, on my back, clutching tightly at my shirt. The other members of my small party were assisting older children and some adult female Malays. An adult male worker joined in and helped too.

As we made our way back to the safety of our vehicles, I could feel the flow of the flood waters pressing against my legs. There was one moment in the gloom when I saw what I thought was a piece of coir matting floating towards me turn out to be a raft of large ants. I twisted my body out of the way and the raft of ants floated past me by a few inches. I did not relish the idea of hundreds of large ants making a landfall on me. It was dark by the time we reached the trucks. Helping the women wade through the water, and with the children on our backs took time. The rescued Malays were most grateful, and thanked us. The Civil Authorities then took the families away to a safe place for the night. There was nothing more for us to do so we made our way back to Batu Gajah. In camp I soon undressed and got under the shower to wash off the muddy swamp water, and was surprised that no leeches had attached themselves to me.

I later received a nice letter of thanks from the Perak State Government.

One day in February we held a parade for the farewell visit of our Brigade Commander, Brigadier C R Campbell Hardy. We were smart in our olive green shirts and shorts. The unit identification white lanyard around our right shoulder and white garter tabs in our stocking tops. The Brigadier inspected the Troop and then called it to gather around him under the shade of a big tree in the camp grounds. He addressed the Troop and thanked all ranks for their efforts in dealing with the bandits.

On St David's Day, 1 March 1951, the Bishop of Singapore and his party, while visiting 42 Commando RM, paid 'B' Troop a visit, which went well. During the visit they were invited into the Officers' Mess, and the Sergeants' Mess where they met Sergeant Wilson, two other sergeants and myself. They inquired of us how were things at home, and how were we coping with the strain?

Another nice touch was when Mrs Madoc, wife of the Commanding Officer of 42 Commando RM, Lt Col R Madoc, came to our camp with two other senior officers' wives, to give the boys a tea party and to have a chat. In the shade of the veranda of the Rest House, they covered some service tables with table cloths and laid out sandwiches and cakes. Soft drinks and tea were also provided. This event went down very well with

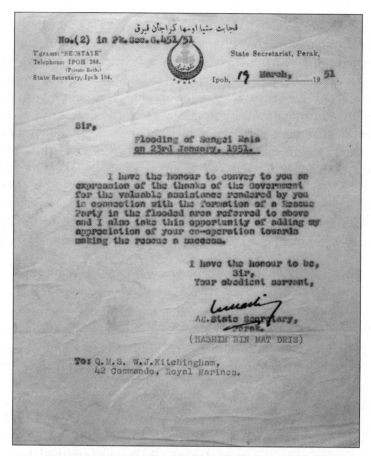

فجابت ستبا اوسها كراجان فيرق

No.(2) in Pk.Sec.G.451/51.

T'grams: "SECSTATE"
Telephone: IPOH 388.
(Private Exch.)
State Secretary, Ipoh 184.

State Secretariat, Perak,

Ipoh, 19 March, 19 51.

Sir,

Flooding of Sungei Raia
on 23rd January, 1951.

I have the honour to convey to you an
expression of the thanks of the Government
for the valuable assistance rendered by you
in connection with the formation of a Rescue
Party in the flooded area referred to above
and I also take this opportunity of adding my
appreciation of your co-operation towards
making the rescue a success.

I have the honour to be,
Sir,
Your obedient servant,

Ag. State Secretary,
Perak.

(HASHIM BIN MAT DRIS)

To: Q.M.S. W.J.Kitchingham,
42 Commando, Royal Marines.

Letter of thanks from the State Secretariat Perak, Malaya. March 1951

all ranks, and was a talking point weeks later.

When sections were stood down an armoured truck would take men, who so wished, to Ipoh for a few hours break. Football matches were often arranged with other Troops or local Malay teams. The Kinta Club, a local club, offered our Officers and SNCOs the facilities of their Club House. In the evenings, operational requirements allowing, we would walk the short distance from camp to relax at their bar.

The most sad duty of 'B' Troop was to provide a security guard around the perimeter of Batu Gajah Cemetery when the military funerals took place. I remember the funeral of a Sergeant who was serving in another Troop, he lost his life when out on patrol. Not long afterwards there was the funeral of a Troop Commander who was shot dead leading his Troop against a group of bandits.

42 Commando RM pressed on with its activities against the bandits. Morale was high in 'B' Troop. Seven members of the Troop including our Troop Commander were awarded military decorations in recognition of their leadership and successful actions against the bandits.

Good information was coming in from the local population so that by the end of June 1951 'B' Troop had handed over to the Civil Authorities 27 bandits killed or captured. The results of the actions of the other troops of 42 Commando RM were, 'A' Troop 6, 'X' Troop 11 and 'Y' Troop 12.

My tour of duty of two and a half years was drawing to a close, and on the 5 July I left 'B' Troop, 42 Commando RM and travelled south by train down through Malaya to Singapore with a group of marines who were also due for repatriation. The train journey was miserably slow with many stops and starts. The night seemed so long; we just sat and whiled away the hours as the train trundled on its way. At last the train arrived in Singapore and we embarked, with many other servicemen, in a troopship and sailed for England.

A few weeks later, in August, there was a redeployment of the security forces in the area. 45 Commando RM took over from 'B' Troop at Batu Gajah and 42 Commando RM moved a few miles south to Selangor.

Chapter 9

45 Commando RM
Malta, Cyprus and Aden

I had been serving at the Infantry Training Centre, Royal Marines, Lympstone, Devon for the past few years in the Weapon Training Department as a Quartermaster Sergeant Instructor when my turn for an overseas tour came up. I joined 45 Commando RM at Imtafa Barracks in Malta on the 3 February 1957, and was appointed Troop Sergeant Major of 'B' Troop.

Patricia and I agreed to take advantage of the accompanied families' scheme of a two and a half years tour. So, with our three small daughters she vacated our married quarters at 19 Trafalgar Road, Lympstone on the 25 March, and travelled to Malta in the troopship *Empire Ken*, arriving in Grand Harbour on the 2 April 1957.

I had been granted a few days leave from Tripoli, where the Commando was on exercises, to meet my family and to see them settled into their new home. I found accommodation in Melfar Flats, in the Paceville district. The flat was new, in the process of being furnished, and the Maltese owner was very kind in letting us move in.

I then rejoined 'B' Troop back at Waterfall Camp, in the desert south of Tripoli. 45 Commando RM had gone to Tripoli on the 12 March for a period of desert training, returning to Malta on the 26 April. The training went well and for a short spell we had some rain.

When the unit returned to Malta we had a nice time with our families, meeting many friends whom we knew from Lympstone. We visited St Paul's Bay where the Saint was said to have been shipwrecked, and many other interesting places in Malta.

The Commandant General Royal Marines, Lieutenant General C R Hardy, came out from London to inspect the unit. On the 21 May there was a full ceremonial parade and march past at Imtafa Barracks, and I was very pleased when he presented me with the Long Service and Good Conduct Medal during the parade.

45 Commando RM had now received a warning order to move to Cyprus, so we got busy preparing our stores and loaded the LST. We sailed on the 25 May, arriving at Cyprus in the early morning of the 29th - the Royal Navy's faithful old Landing Ships Tank, LSTs, Reggio and Striker were still operating from Malta, carrying the Commando Units around the Mediterranean area.

Upon disembarkation, the various Troops moved off in their own vehicle convoys for the new location at Platres, 3700 feet up in the Troodos Mountains, where we would be for the next four months. We were on the alert in case we were ambushed

The author receiving the Long Service and Good Conduct Medal from the Commandant General Royal Marines, Lieutenant General Sir Campbell Hardy KCB CBE DSO, at Imtafa Barracks Malta 21 May 1957

as we weaved our way up the twisting mountain road, leaving the heat of the coastal plain behind us.

As 'B' Troop's trucks approached Platres we came to a clearing where helicopter training had been taking place by a Troop which had been in the advance party, but, as we slowly drove past the scene I saw on the ground the wreckage of a 'chopper'. I asked a sergeant, who was standing nearby with his section of marines, what had happened. He said there had been an accident, a Marine had been seriously injured and a colleague of mine, Quartermaster Sergeant Graham Casey, Troop Sergeant Major of 'E' Troop, had died of injuries received when the helicopter crashed to the ground. This was sad news indeed to start a tour of duty.

We drove on into Platres, unloaded our trucks and settled the Troop into its quarters. A number of hotels were used for accommodation. In addition to those used by the troops, there was one for the Sergeants' Mess, and another as the Officers' Mess up the road a little way, not far from the Police Station.

Next morning, the 30 May, 45 Commando RM took over operational duties from 40 Commando RM. Notwithstanding the accident, helicopter training for all ranks recommenced. One of the skills we practised was climbing down a rope hanging from the helicopter while it hovered about fifteen feet above the sloping ground.

For the next few weeks 'B' Troop operated from Platres. We carried out cordon and search operations in company with elements of the Cyprus Police and Special Branch. Army tracker dogs and their handlers were often in attendance.

Platres was a small township with its houses built on terraces in the lush wooded mountain side. There were gardens and fruit trees which were supplied

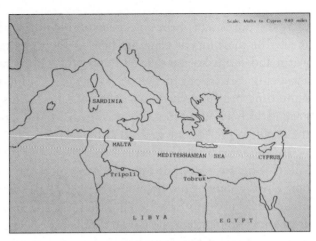

45 Commando RM Malta and Cyprus

with fresh Troodos mountain water from a system of concrete lined water channels. Dessert grapes hung in large bunches from overhead supports, and the foliage of the vines in summer provided shade from the sun. We soon got to know the Gift Shop at the road junction and, of course, Kosta's Bar. The local drinks were Cyprus brandy sours, Cyprus sherry and Keo beer. A nice dessert wine was Commanderier St John.

In July 1957 'B' Troop set up a base camp in the sheds of the Keo Wine Factory at Perapedhi for a week. The large vats were not in use, but there was the smell of wine making in the air. The time was spent in laying a road block at Kilani, and searching all vehicles. Marines patrolling the area on foot found two prepared ambush positions on ground overlooking horseshoe bends on the mountain roads.

I had a look at one site. It had four firing positions where plunging fire could be directed at vehicles on the road below. Naturally we kept these positions, and others, in mind when using the road, sometimes sending a foot patrol over the high ground to cover or lay an ambush on the position before our vehicles went through.

Time soon came for 'B' Troop to relieve the Troop stationed at the Troodos Camp further up the mountain, at 5500 feet. Nearby was Mount Olympus at just over 6400 feet. Up here the mountain air was fresh and the smell of the resin from the many pine trees, which grew all over this area, hung on the air.

It was at this camp where the army tracker dogs for the area were kennelled. There were over a dozen dogs, Labradors, Alsatians and Doberman Pinschers, all in the care of an army sergeant and a section of dog handlers.

We had an incident in camp one morning in August 1957. For security reasons, so that bandits could not raid civilian explosive stores, we held in a secure magazine a supply of dynamite in boxes for the Amiandos Asbestos Mine which was only a few miles away. The dynamite, when called for by the mine manager, was loaded onto one of our lorries and delivered under armed escort to the mine, for immediate use.

My Troop Commander had informed me earlier that a number of boxes of dynamite were required by the mine before noon that day. So I ordered a marine to carry the boxes out of the magazine and load the vehicle while I adjusted the stock sheet. The morning, as usual up here in the mountains at this time of the year, was warm and sunny so the marine removed his shirt whilst he worked. As the last box was being carried out of the magazine, the marine started to let the box slip, at the same time brushing furiously at his chest with his free hand and stamping at the ground with a booted foot. He was unable to hold on to the box with one hand, and the explosives fell to the ground at his feet.

In true sergeant major terms I enquired what that performance was all about. He said that he was sorry but thought a scorpion had stung him when he picked up the box. I had a look at his chest and sure enough something had stung him, so I sent him off to our camp Sick Berth Attendant for medical attention. He was, however, after a few hours none the worse for his experience, except that he might break out in a cold sweat at the thought of a box of dynamite exploding at his feet. However there was no chance of that, the dynamite required detonators, and they were stored separately.

Some of our marines were not keen on being in the asbestos mine area. A newspaper cutting had been passed round the camp pointing out the health hazard from breathing asbestos dust.

45 Commando RM left Cyprus in the last week of September for Malta. And a few weeks later we were off to Sardinia in the LSTs for a large scale amphibious exercise. Mosquitoes created havoc with most of us, even though each man had his container of insect/mosquito repellent and face nets. The mosquito bites caused the faces of two of our marines to swell so much that the lads could hardly see. To add to our discomfort it rained quite a lot, and we were wet from top to toe, even though we were wearing our poncho capes.

After the exercise the unit, on its way back to Malta, called at Sicily where we had an afternoon sightseeing in the ancient city of Palermo.

45 Commando RM was then back in Malta where we spent Christmas 1957 and the New Year. The Sergeants' Mess laid on a party for the children, complete with Father Christmas and a sack of presents for the young ones. It was a happy time for us with our families.

Our two daughters, Beverley and Elizabeth were attending the Army Children's School at St Andrew's Barracks, not far from where we lived in Paceville.

While I was away from Malta, Patricia had found a first floor flat which she liked. So we moved out of the ground floor accommodation in Melfar Flats into Attard Flats, just a few yards away.

The wives and families had developed a good community spirit. And when we were away from Malta the unit families' liaison officer kept our wives up to date with unit news, and helped deal with any problems that arose with our families.

The usual desert training period was upon us again. So it was off to Tripoli on the 18 March 1958 but, because of political unrest in the island, we had to return to Malta for internal security duties on the 15 April.

45 Commando RM moved to Cyprus at the end of July 1958 for a five month period of security duties in the Troodos area. For a few weeks 'B' Troop and Support Troop operated from the Commando outstation at the Pinewood Valley Hotel, near the village of Pedhoulas about 3600 feet on the north side of the Troodos Mountains.

The Officer Commanding 'S' Troop, being the senior officer of our location, had called a meeting - we knew them as 'O' Groups, the 'O' standing for 'Orders'. He said

Two members of the unit shop staff at the camp entrance among the pine trees at Troodos, close to the summit of Mount Olympus, Cyprus 1957

he had received a report from Commando Headquarters that a forest fire had broken out among the pine trees on a mountain range a few miles away to the north west of our location. Headquarters had been called upon for troops to assist the Cyprus Forestry Commission to fight it. 'B' and 'S' Troops, with local forestry workers as guides, would approach the fire from the north. Further units would move in from other directions. In total about 600 men were involved. Each man would carry a shovel to dig fire breaks to stop ground fire from creeping and spreading. A few weapons were to be taken in case terrorists were encountered.

It was the middle Friday in August 1958. Our vehicles took us as far as the forest tracks would allow. We then had to walk for about two hours in the pre-dawn light, scrambling up steep ridges and down small valleys to get to the fire. [Because of the very serious consequences of being caught in a forest fire all ranks, on joining the Commando in Cyprus, were required to attend a forest fire fighting course. 45 Commando RM had been called on in the past to give assistance to the Cyprus Forestry Commission in fighting forest fires in the general area of the Troodos Mountains. In fact, in June 1956, during a large scale cordon and search operation involving Army and Royal Marine forces a forest fire started which soon got out of control and claimed the lives of nineteen Army servicemen.]

Our local forestry guide was now leading 'B' Troop around and ahead of the fire, and down a wooded valley towards it. We were about 2500 feet up in the mountains. As we moved along I noticed we had just passed a burnt out ridge, the ground and tree trunks were blackened and still smouldering. 'B' Troop was being guided to a position further along the line of the fire, and was out of sight somewhere ahead of us.

We were moving in single file down a wooded re-entrant, the Troop Commander and the guide were leading and the sections following. I was at the rear with the Troop Clerk who was carrying one of the troop radios. From our position at the rear,

A Cypriot forest worker and members of 'B' Troop 45 Commando RM hastily moving onto a burnt out ridge in a forest fire, August 1958, Cyprus

and more importantly at this time at the top of the valley, we could see the line of the fire and our men as we moved down the tree covered slope. My reaction was that the guide had got it wrong; we were in the wrong position. If the wind changed direction the Troop, being ahead of the fire, would be in serious danger. Normally here in the early mornings there is little or no wind, but as the mornings wear on, and the day gets hotter, the wind increases in strength and blows in from the sea.

I immediately instructed the Troop Clerk to call up the Troop Commander on the radio as I wanted to report the danger I saw. As we made contact the wind started to change direction and increased in strength, blowing the smoke up the valley towards us. Then I saw the flames advancing towards the head of our column. I shouted an order to the sections to follow me, and moved sideways to the safety of the burnt out ridge about seventy-five yards away.

The guide and the Troop Commander realized what was happening and immediately turned round. It was a good job we were fairly fit men. Even so, the flames were advancing faster than we could run, and gaining on us. The guide and the Troop Commander, being at the head and leading the Troop, had further to run. Three young marines who were close by snatched them to safety as the inferno, a crown fire, raced up the wooded valley with the speed and noise of an express train. We could feel the heat of the flames as they set fire to everything in their path that would burn.

Once on the burnt out ridge I ordered a roll call by sections as I feared we may have had casualties. Thankfully, after the Section Sergeants had reported in, I was able to inform the Troop Commander that we had all made the safety of the burnt out ridge.

We were coughing from the effect of the smoke, and rested for some time while we got our breath back. Then we saw a pall of smoke go up from an adjacent valley and hoped that no one was caught in it. 'A' or 'S' Troop were somewhere in the area.

A helicopter went overhead, and shortly afterwards Commando HQ called up on the radio for a situation report, which was given. We were then instructed to make for a rendezvous point where transport would be waiting to take us back to our camp. During the early morning I had been checking our position very closely on the map as we made our way into the area and I was quite sure of where we were. In this kind of country it would take us about an hour and a half to walk the short distance over some very rough ground to the transport.

At the RV point we met up with 'A' Troop, and learned that they had been in the adjacent valley that we saw go up in smoke and flames. They, like us, had had to run for it, their Troop Sergeant Major suffered burns to his hands. It had been a narrow escape for both 'A' and 'B' Troops.

During the troubled times in Cyprus we never knew just what the next day would bring. The lovely summer days with the smell of the pine trees hanging on the Troodos mountain air were often marred by terrorists' activities.

One morning a police Landrover, with two uniformed police officers on secondment duty to the Cyprus Police from their United Kingdom Police Force, was ambushed on the twisting mountain road north of Platres. Both officers were killed. One officer was within a few weeks of his return to the UK on completion of his tour of duty.

They used to visit our camps whenever they were in the area and have a chat over a cup of tea in the Sergeants' Mess. When their vehicle was recovered I had a look at it. The metal side panels were punctured with quite a number of what looked like .45 inch calibre Thompson sub-machine gun bullet holes.

The Middle East Shooting Championships, under service conditions, were held on the Army ranges at Dhekelia in November 1958. Many units of the three armed services participated. Shortly before the meeting, our Commanding Officer gave us time to do some training shoots to be able to select a good team. It paid off, 45 Commando RM won just about every event which pleased our Commanding Officer and everyone else in the unit.

Our time in Cyprus was drawing to a close and, on the 15 December, we moved back to Malta for Christmas. However, the new year, 1959, saw the unit on internal security duties in Malta.

My two and a half years' tour of duty with 45 Commando RM came to an end and I was to be posted back to Lympstone. So, on the 10 June 1959 I flew back to the United Kingdom with my family. Married quarters were available for us to move into at Lamplough Road, Exmouth, not far from the camp. My wife and daughters enjoyed their time living in Malta, making many friends.

I had been serving at the Infantry Training Centre, Royal Marines, Lympstone for the past three years when my turn for an overseas posting came up. So, on the 8 September 1962, I was one of a small number of Royal Marines who were drafted to 45 Commando RM, which was stationed in Aden. The base camp was actually a few miles away at Little Aden.

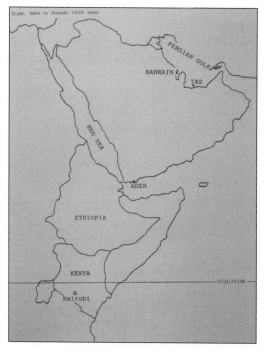

45 Commando RM Aden

Because of the nature of the posting the tour of duty would be for twelve months. So my family would be staying in our house at Exmouth.

The Royal Marines Drafting Office had a busy time keeping up with the turn round of personnel for foreign service. It was an on-going task meeting the repatriation dates. Sometimes the draft was only a few in number, such as ours, other times there might be a dozen marines or more.

We flew out from Stansted airport and fifteen hours later landed at RAF Khormaksar, Aden at sunrise, having made a refuelling stop on the way. However, even at this early hour the heat of Aden greeted me as I left the aircraft like a blast of hot air from a hot oven when the door is opened.

Two RM drivers with their Landrovers met us, and after we collected our baggage we headed along the Causeway and round the bay to Little Aden. On passing the Federal Capital buildings at Al Ittihad, our driver pointed to a small area of disturbed sandy soil on the left hand side of the road and said, in a matter of fact way, "That's where a mine exploded yesterday!"

As we approached Little Aden we could see the BP oil refinery on our right, with a tongue of flame coming from tall gas flare-off pipes, and the smell of oil and gas hung on the air. At night the flame from the flare-off pipes cast a glow over a wide area, including the camp site. Our accommodation was in the air conditioned, prefabricated huts of the BP oil refinery construction camp.

I reported my arrival to the Regimental Sergeant Major who said that a room was ready for me in the Sergeants' Mess block. I washed, shaved and generally tidied myself up and then reported to him at the orderly room. After seeing the Commanding Officer I was appointed Company Sergeant Major of 'Y' Company.

The Commando, to meet operational needs at this time, was changing from the old five fighting Troop formation to one of three Rifle Companies, plus Support and HQ Companies. Training was under way to get things right in the new formation, and we soon got ourselves used to the changes.

Political agitators were causing unrest in the local population and, on the 24 September 1962, 'Y' Company was deployed in Aden on internal security duties. I was with our Company Commander and Company HQ supported by No 4 Troop at Maalla Police Station; and we were in radio contact with the rest of the company. No 5

Troop was about six miles away at Sheikh Othman, and No 6 Troop was about two and a half miles away at RAF Steamer Point. There was a certain amount of agitation and tension in the crowds in the streets. However, as time went by and the Civil Authorities became satisfied that matters had cooled down our Company Commander received orders for us to return to our base at Little Aden.

During the period 10 to 16 November 1962, we were engaged on a very serious large scale exercise, 'Hollow Laugh' - when I looked back at the exercise, and read of the political aspects at the time, I felt someone in staff planning must have had a sense of humour. However, it went very well, more of an operational patrol in force, than an ordinary exercise.

The Army was in support with a squadron of Centurion tanks and scout cars. There were Royal Engineers and a mobile vehicle workshop. The exercise started with 45 Commando RM making an amphibious landing on a beach near Shuqra, some one hundred miles east of Aden. We headed inland on foot a short distance until our company vehicles caught up with us. Then the whole force of about 1000 men moved off, almost due north, for Lodar about fifty miles inland. We got wet from the beach landing but the hot sun soon dried our clothing and boots. As we left the coastal plain and moved into the high ground, the landscape took on a character of its own. There were high craggy peaks, rocks and bolders. Stones littered the surface of the sand and the dust was as fine as powder. The vehicles were following a traditional route from the coast to Lodar, but the track was unbelievably rough. I overheard some marines, who had been with the unit for some months, declaring that it was worse than the Dhala road. I was to recall their comments later when 'Y' Company went to Dhala, I agreed with them. The vehicles were having a tough time of it, the strength of their chassis being tested, and chunks of rubber were torn off the tyres on the rough surface of the track. The terrain got worse as we went through the mountain pass making riding in the back of the trucks very unpleasant.

On the second day, as we neared our destination, 'Y' Company was ordered to ride on the Centurion tanks and move ahead of the force. The dust was getting everywhere. I tied a cloth over my nose and mouth, and hung onto the tank. The air behind us looked like a sand storm was blowing. We were ordered to stop well short of Lodar and deploy whilst the remainder of the force came up. Inquisitive locals held back some distance, watching us and no doubt discussing the event.

Early morning stop Aden 1962

Our Company Quartermaster Sergeant (CQMS) was marvellous in keeping up with the supply of drinking water and food. Each man carried his own ration pack and two water bottles, and there were canvas water containers - chuggels, which kept the water fairly cool through evaporation, strapped to the sides of the vehicles. The water sterilizing tablets sometimes tainted the drinking water but it is accepted when one is thirsty. The logistics of supplying an armed force on the move with ammunition, fuel, water, food and equipment from a rear supply base right up to the troops on the ground is a major task, and requires detailed planning and co-ordination.

Our whole force after a few hours at Lodar started the return journey. The Fleet Air Arm joined in with Scimitar and twin boomed Sea Vixen aircraft from the Royal Navy carrier, *Ark Royal*. As part of the exercise they flew sorties over us, contour flying around the high peaks and diving on our large convoy of tanks and vehicles as we made our way through the narrow passes. The Fleet Air Arm pilots showed off their skill with some low flying and no doubt enjoyed themselves.

As soon as we returned to the coast it was back to camp at Little Aden for a good wash down under the shower, and then into a comfortable bed in our air conditioned quarters for a few hours' sleep. The unit was now on a twenty-four hour stand-down.

During a stand-down the Sergeants' Mess usually held a social evening, inviting members of Sergeants' Messes of other units in the area, or Chief Petty Officers and Petty Officers from Royal Navy ships in Aden. A number of party games were played; darts, liar dice and card games. Drinking the gallon of beer was popular. Eight members of each mess team would line up against a row of tables laden with glasses of beer and, on the signal 'Go!' each member of the team would, in turn, drink his pint of beer as quickly as possible; the team with the shortest time being the winner. I have little doubt that a fair number of visitors did not remember walking out of our mess door at the end of the evening to return to their units. It was all good fun, and there must have been some sore heads in the morning after.

One morning our Company Commander, who had been at the Commanding Officer's briefing, called a meeting of 'Y' Company Lieutenants and SNCOs, and said that we were to get ready as soon as possible for an airlift with full fighting equipment and stores. The next few hours saw us putting into effect a well-practised routine, and on the 14th February 1963 we flew off to Bahrain in RAF Argosy aircraft. On our arrival Army transport vehicles took us to the 1st Parachute Regiment Camp on the outskirts of the city. We then spent a few days in sandy defensive positions under a very hot sun - Bahrain is an island in the Persian Gulf, about 300 miles south of Kuwait, where a rapid deployment of UK forces took place in early July 1961.

We were then withdrawn to camp for a clean-up. The unit later embarked in Royal Navy ships for an amphibious landing exercise on the Island of Yas in the Persian Gulf, just off the coast of the Trucial States. During our exercise on this low lying, bare, sandy island we came across some friendly local fishermen, who laughed and must have thought us completely mad. Then it was back to Bahrain by ship and a return flight to Aden on the 27th following quite a busy two weeks.

The time came for 'Y' Company to relieve the company at the military camp near the Arab community of Dhala. The township, which lies a few miles south of the border with the Yemen, commands an ancient and important trade route from the Port of Aden to the interior.

The road journey north from Little Aden took about nine hours to cover a distance of just over eighty miles, rising from sea level to an elevation of over 5000 feet. We started early in the morning, just before sun up, and made good time during the early part of the journey as we drove inland from the coastal plain. A routine stop was made at the small Arab village of Thumier before we moved into the foothills and mountain pass, which led to Dhala. I had a photograph taken of myself with our convoy during the rest period at Thumier, with the local white-washed fort, manned by Federal National Guards, in the background.

The tarmacadam road had long given way to a stony track, which got worse during the latter part of our journey as we moved through the steep and twisting Khuraybah Pass. The troops had to walk some sections and scout the route for ambushes before the convoy moved on, even though Federal National Guards had been posted at key positions to cover our movement.

Above: Dhala Camp - Aden 1963

Right: The author (on the left) walking past tents in Dhala Camp with a colleague 1963

Our camp, which was a tented affair, was established on a bare ridge of the Dhala plateau. A dry stone wall with a barbed wire fence surrounded our camp. Nearby was the Aden Protectorate Levies Camp, and in the background some high ground with a peak, Jebel Jihaf, overshadowed the area.

I travelled the Dhala road five times, and on one occasion I flew up from the small airstrip at the rear of Little Aden in a single-engined engined aircraft with two other marines. The pilot had not long arrived in Aden and this was his first trip to Dhala. Although he had his map and flew on a compass bearing he kept asking me, "What did the Dhala airstrip look like'?" The two marines and I kept a look out for the Dhala Camp, and as soon as we spotted it we were able to point out the dusty earth airstrip below. It must have been something of a surprise to him. There was a ridge of high ground near the airstrip, which itself was at about 5500 feet. The pilot then told us, rather curtly, to 'shut up' as he wanted to concentrate on his approach and landing. Just as well I thought, as he set the plane down. Our approach had been noticed in camp and we were met by the duty section which had driven the short distance from camp to the airstrip.

The Dhala airstrip was used by the service aircraft for flying in our camp supplies. A section of marines under a sergeant went out daily to search the area around the airstrip to make sure it was safe for the planes to land. Mail was always eagerly awaited and very quickly sorted and distributed.

We tried to use the airstrip one night to fly out a local inhabitant who had received a bullet wound and who was in urgent need of hospital treatment. A radio message to Headquarters brought an aircraft overhead in a very short period of time. The pilot requested the landing strip to be illuminated. So the drivers switched on the headlights of the few vehicles we had, and two sergeants and I set out a line of trip flares. We could hear the plane circling in the dark sky above us. Without doubt, the pilot was very brave to consider a landing. The rim of the surrounding high ground, hidden in the darkness, made the attempt much too dangerous and the pilot returned to Aden. Throughout the night our camp doctor and sick berth attendant worked tirelessly to give the youth all the attention at their disposal but sadly he died before sun up.

'Y' Company was engaged in patrolling the Dhala area and the surrounding countryside. The RAF pilots flew air patrols along the Aden side of the border with the Yemen in their Hawker Hunter jet fighters, passing close to our camp. On one occasion I took a series of photographs showing the camp with the aircraft flying past in the background.

At a lonely Federal National Guard outpost, a few miles north of our camp, we had an armed observation post manned by a couple of marines and an NCO, with binoculars and a radio. From this lofty position they were able to keep the great waddi, many hundreds of feet below, under observation.

On one occasion I was with a patrol which carried supplies to them. Each of us carried at least 50 lbs on a manpack frame, and of course we had to carry our weapons with us. Landrovers took the patrol as far as vehicles could go, then it was on foot to climb a further 500 feet up a donkey track. I was carrying one of the 4 gallon jerry cans full of drinking water, and could hear the water slopping about in the can as we made our way to the top of the Jebel. On arrival we were greeted by a couple of Arabs from the very small community living up here.

While we unloaded our stores my eyes gave away my surprise at the sight of a man shuffling towards us. He was chained hand and foot and carried what looked like a cannon-ball to which the chains were attached. The Federal National Guardsman, who noticed my reaction, explained that the man had committed a very serious crime and this was his punishment. The prisoner had to look after himself, and he was not likely to get far if he tried to escape.

The second week of May 1963 saw 45 Commando RM on the move once again, an air portability exercise to Kenya for two weeks. The Unit took off from the Khormaksar airfield, Aden, in a number of aircraft of the Royal Air Force Transport Command for Nairobi, 1000 miles to the south of Aden. 'Y' Company were in Britannia aircraft.

We landed at dawn and while we waited in the airport lounge for our equipment to be unloaded from the aircraft and put into road transport, some kind local people served us with piping hot fresh coffee - I have little doubt it was Kenyan coffee, it was delicious. At this time of the early morning it was a most thoughtful welcome to Kenya.

Despite the fact that we were now just south of the equator, we experienced a welcome change in climatic conditions, from the shimmering hot desert sands of Aden at sea level to the clear air of the scrubby brown grasslands of the Kenyan Highlands near Nairobi, at an elevation of over 5000 feet. This elevation of Nairobi airport was an important factor in determining aircraft payloads for take-off on our return flights. Extra weight was the last thing the pilots wanted during take-off at this height above sea level. Someone wanted to take back to Aden a number of sandbags filled with soil with which to enrich a mess flower garden, but the pilots quickly put an end to this foolishness.

The road transport took us along some hard packed reddish-brown earth roads to an area a few miles north of Nairobi where we would carry out Company and Commando attack exercises. Mount Kenya, which could be seen in the distance rising to over 17,000 feet, acted as a back drop to our exercises.

The days were warm and the nights cool but our service sleeping bags kept us snug at night. Some nights were spent in the open in slit trenches which we had dug a few hours previously, but during the short rest period we had a few nights in some Army marquees.

During this break in our training programme we had some time to ourselves. The men were warned not go swimming in the rivers or pools, or to drink the water as the risk of infection from a very nasty tropical disease, bilharzia, was very high.

I went with a group of 'Y' Company marines in two of our small trucks into the nearby foothills and came upon a small country market by the side of the earth track. Nearby was a cluster of round huts with grass thatch roofs. The villagers were friendly people, but I found it difficult to understand what they were saying. The children, as children nearly always seem to do wherever we were, soon came up to us and looked us over. They jumped around us touching our uniforms and clambered over our vehicles. It was heart-warming to see their little faces light up with delight as we gave them our ration pack sweets and bars of chocolate. We waved 'Goodbye' as we left and received friendly waves in return from the adults as well as the children.

On our way back to the training area we came across elephant droppings and tracks. We hoped to see the animals but no luck, their tracks went off in a different direction. We had to be careful and check our position on the map of the area to get back on course for the training area.

With close on 600 men digging slit trenches in the ground and carrying out fieldcraft exercises it was not surprising, therefore, that little wild life was to be seen, but there were snakes. I had seen four or five during the first week, two were at least five feet long. In fact, during the approach phase of our final Commando attack exercise, a marine in the company on our left was bitten by a puff adder. Vital information is usually passed from marine to marine with surprising speed by using sign language. I have little doubt that everyone in the whole Commando knew of this incident within seconds. Extra attention was, therefore, paid to what might lie on the ground in our path. No doubt most of us felt a little shudder run through our bodies at the thought of receiving a snake bite.

The unlucky marine was quickly given the appropriate snake bite treatment by the unit sick berth attendants. Fortunately, a light aircraft was available and was used to fly the injured man to Nairobi for further treatment. He recovered from his ordeal and has a good party story to tell. In all my overseas service, even in Malaya, he was the only marine I knew of to be bitten by a snake.

When the final exercise ended the unit spent a few days in the Army barracks in Nairobi before the return flight to Aden. As you might expect our priorities were; a nice wash down under a hot shower, a change of clothing from our   rucksacks, a cool beer at the Sergeants' Mess bar followed by a meal, and a good night's sleep.

The following day a drive through a nearby game reserve had been arranged for those who wished to see the Kenyan wild life at close hand. Our group of SNCOs made up two mini-bus loads. The plan was to find some lions and photograph them from the safety of the vehicles. The drivers said they knew where to find a pride and we set off along a rough track for miles through the scrub and grassland of the reserve. We were unlucky, there were no lions to be seen and very few other animals were in the area. I began to wonder why I came along. We had already spent two weeks living rough in the training area, and I knew well enough what the terrain looked like.

Then as we came over a rise in the ground we saw two cheetahs less than ten yards ahead of us, moving leisurely along the side of the dirt track. The driver stopped the vehicle and told us to be quiet and watch. We sat in the enclosed mini bus for about ten minutes looking out of the windows at the scene. First one cheetah would sit on its haunches with its round head just above the light brown scrubby grass surveying the ground ahead while the second animal made a stealthy flanking move to the right and, as soon as it in turn took up an observation position the first cheetah then moved forward, and so they carried on. This pair of cheetahs took no notice of us in the vehicle as they searched for prey. Eventually they went out of sight in the undulating ground.

As we moved on, my mind went back to the time when I was a schoolboy on a visit to a zoo. Although it was educational to see the various animals I did not like to see them pacing up and down in their cages. We were fortunate indeed to watch these two cheetahs in their natural habitat; a cage was no place for such fine animals. During my various postings overseas I had a number of opportunities to go game hunting with SNCOs but I never wished to shoot and kill a wild animal for sport or fun.

We were back in the Army barracks by late afternoon, and orders came to prepare for the return flight. So, on the 26th after our military stores were loaded into the aircraft we boarded the plane. The RAF Britannia took the full length of the runway here at Nairobi to get airborne, we were almost willing it into the air. All onboard soon settled down to a rather boring flight back to Aden.

In Little Aden during the off duty periods we had a number of activities available. We could go swimming in the sea from a beach which was well protected by a shark net. There was a sandy golf course of a few holes. Oil was sprayed on the 'greens' to consolidate the sand thus giving some kind of a surface for the putts to be made. And, as part of keep fit routine, there was jogging in the late afternoon.

After dark the camp's open-air cinema was popular. The evening's programme usually opened with a short cartoon film. The antics of the characters sometimes drew service language comments from the audience, raising a laugh and helping to relax the audience.

I was posted back to Lympstone in June 1963.

Chapter 10
United Kingdom units

The two years following my return to Stonehouse Barracks, from my sea service, in January 1947 was a busy period for me. It was time that I should get a specialist qualification. The Corps had a number of specialist branches, such as Clerks, Cooks, Radio Operators, Vehicle Mechanics and Drivers all required for the efficient running of the Corps at home and overseas. There were Physical Training Instructors, Parade Instructors and Small Arms Instructors. I felt my niche was in the Small Arms Branch, so I requested to take a course to become an Instructor.

I was promoted to Sergeant in June, and a few weeks later posted to the Small Arms School Royal Marines at Browndown near Gosport Hants for a Junior Instructors course. Browndown Camp, with the rifle ranges on the shingle beach, was apparently founded about the year 1840 and the Corps is believed to have occupied it in 1880. However, in the mid-1950s the activities of the Small Arms School were transferred to the Infantry Training Centre at Lympstone, Devon.

The lovely summer months of 1947 helped to make an interesting course at Browndown even more enjoyable. After qualifying in October I returned to the West Country being posted to the training staff at the Commando School, Royal Marines at Bickleigh in Devon. Six weeks later, in January 1948, I was drafted to the Depot Royal Marines, Deal, Kent and served in the Weapon Training Department for twelve months. The Depot was busy with the basic training of recruits. As in all training establishments strict discipline was necessary to instil the correct attitude into the minds of the young recruits.

Meanwhile, the Corps was adapting to its new role following the Government Defence Review. It became Corps policy that all ranks should complete a commando course prior to service in the Commando Units, so by the end of the year I was posted to the Commando School again but this time for a conversion course lasting six weeks.

I was in a squad of senior non-commissioned officers from all parts of the Corps, including SNCOs from HM Ships. Not long ago I had served at Bickleigh and knew what was to come. The other SNCOs looked upon it with dismay, very quickly realizing they were not fit men. However, with team work and the steadfast and trusted Commando spirit of 'me and my oppo' all completed the course and were awarded their Green Beret.

It was the winter of 1948-49. A nine mile speed march in ninety minutes in the cold is much to be preferred than in hot weather, but it was with some relief that we got to the end of the endurance march across the chilling, wind-blown, rain soaked bleak expanses of Dartmoor.

I was drafted to 42 Commando RM in March 1949, returning to Stonehouse Barracks in August 1951. After foreign service leave with my family, I again joined the staff at the Depot RM for a few months. Then it was back to Browndown on the 19 January 1952 for a further Small Arms Instructors course.

I well remember the cold, overcast winter's day of the 6 February 1952 when I had to visit the clothing store in Eastney Barracks. Shortly after I got off a bus and was walking along the street towards the Barrack's Main Gate I heard a radio announcement coming from an open doorway of a house that King George VI had died. It was a sad moment. He was a well-loved king who served his country well, through the unwanted dark years of war and into the peace.

On the 6 May 1952 I was promoted to Colour Sergeant and a week later the good news came, I had passed the course and was now a Platoon Weapons Instructor and would be kept on the staff at Browndown.

Towards the end of the summer our Commanding Officer said that he was sending me to the Army Small Arms School Corps unit at Hythe in Kent on a six month instructor exchange arrangement. The main activity at Hythe was the weapon training of young Army officers. It was an invaluable experience for me to work with the Army instructors.

I was back on the staff at Browndown in the spring of 1953. We were running training courses for various service personnel, RN Gunnery Officers, RM Weapon Training Officers, Senior and Junior Non-Commissioned Officers, and live firing demonstrations for staff officers. A few Police Officers attended for small arms firings.

The Coronation Review of the Fleet at Spithead by H M Queen Elizabeth II was held on the 15 June 1953. We had a good view of the various ships of the Fleet which was lying off the shingle beach of the rifle ranges. We had our families for the day, and in the Sergeants' Mess we made quite a party of it all. In fact it was a nice summer's day and there was a party spirit in the whole of the Portsmouth Command area.

Following the change of monarch all our uniform badges and buttons depicting the late King's Crown had to be changed to items showing the St Edward's Crown, adopted by the new Queen.

Patricia and our three young daughters joined me at Browndown. We rented a residential caravan which was sited inside the court yard walls of the disused Stokes Bay fort, a five minute walk from Browndown Camp. A few days later we were joined by another small arms instructor, Peter Willis, with his wife, Anne, and their two young children. They parked their caravan a few yards from our's, it was nice to have their company. These temporary means of accommodation were all very well in the summer months but, as October and November drew on the experience became rather primitive for our wives.

It was while I was serving at Browndown that I had to consider whether to leave the Corps on completion of my first period of service, twelve years, or to re-engage for a further ten years. This would take me to the age of forty years, leading to a service pension. Vacancies for instructors, with good prospects for promotion, were being advertised for the Royal Ulster Constabulary and the Southern Rhodesia Staff Defence Corps. I completed application papers for both. I was well trained and had the necessary experience which would be very useful to these organizations. However, my father and my Commanding Officer persuaded me to continue with my career in the Royal Marines. Promotion to Quartermaster Sergeant Instructor came shortly afterwards, on the 1 October 1953.

I now fully expected a new posting and then, on the 19 November 1953, I was drafted to the Infantry Training Centre Royal Marines, at Lympstone, near Exmouth in Devon. Married families' quarters were available, about one mile from camp, so we occupied one in Trafalgar Road, Lympstone. It was a fairly new and pleasant estate well off the main road, but not too far for our wives to walk down the hill to the Post Office and shops in Lympstone village with the backs of its houses facing the estuary of the river Exe.

There were some fine trees in the area especially on a nearby estate and we soon got used to the calls of owls at night. Patricia and I had never been to this part of the West Country before and looked forward to a pleasant couple of years here.

At the Infantry Training Centre there was a large staff of instructors, working in teams, taking a steady flow of recruit squads through all aspects of their basic training. The programme had a number of subjects including parade work, physical training, small arms and fieldcraft training, all very necessary before the recruits were ready to commence their commando course.

Corps history was an important subject. It helped to cultivate in the minds of the young men that very important quality - Esprit de Corps. This feeling of pride and confidence in one's unit is shared throughout the various ranks of the Corps, from the Commandant General right down to the trained marines in their units no matter where they were serving. This spirit was clearly evident even in the shooting teams when we were competing in inter-service championships at home or abroad. Esprit de Corps has long been fostered in the Royal Marines.

The rifle ranges at Straight Point were on the outskirts of Exmouth, only a few miles from camp, overlooking the waters of the English Channel. Many hours were spent here instructing and coaching recruits in small arms firings prior to going to Dartmoor for co-ordinated field firing exercises with live ammunition. I think the priming and throwing of live hand grenades had a certain risk of accident about it. However, the small arms instructors were highly trained in their craft, and fully qualified to conduct live ammunition training. Lookouts were always posted as the safety regulations had to be observed, not only for the benefit of the servicemen but also for any member of the public who might stray into the danger zone.

In the fields adjacent to the ranges at Straight Point were a few holiday caravans, the Sandy Bay Caravan site. Over the years we saw it develop into a large holiday centre. In summer the sight of young lady holiday makers was a source of distraction. No doubt some of the instructors and range staff visited the holiday camp during off duty hours meeting the girls and developing friendships.

One of our friends, Sergeant Roger Smith, was the Range Warden at Straight Point. During his tenure of duty he lived with his wife, Phyllis, and family in the range warden's quarters on a rather exposed site just inside the main gate to the ranges. They must have felt the full force of the wind and lashing rain when a south west gale was blowing in from the sea.

Another training area was up on Woodbury Common. Here among the trees, scrub and bracken the recruits learned their fieldcraft. They also had practical experience in constructing a bivouac from whatever materials were at hand, bracken was often used. If the shelter was well made the recruits would be fairly comfortable and sleep soundly, otherwise they had a bad night.

I served at Lympstone for three periods, first from 1953 to 1957 and then, following our return from 45 Commando RM in Malta in 1959 until 1962. The third period was for a few months in 1963 after my return from Aden.

During our second period we occupied quarters at Lamplough Road on the outskirts of Exmouth. There was a nice community spirit among the service families living there; a number were old friends. Later we bought a nice sized family house in Waverley Road, Exmouth, so that our four daughters could each have their own room.

At the Training Centre there were members of staff who had completed their terms of engagement in the Corps, and went into civilian life. Some took on running pubs or guest houses locally. Some moved to other parts of the United Kingdom or abroad and we lost contact with them. I knew of three persons, whom I had served with, who took Holy Orders. One had been a major and now was known as Father Donald Peyton-Jones. He had been appointed to the local parish in the Featherbed Lane area close to our home in Exmouth and often called on us. My wife and I were very pleased that he conducted the church service when our two older daughters Beverley and Elizabeth were confirmed. He was often seen in his leather sandals and wearing a brown cassock, sitting astride his horse as he rode around the parish visiting his parishioners.

Chapter 11
Competition Shooting and Bisley

I found in my early teens that I had a natural ability for rifle shooting. My father used to take me to his air gun club in Dundonald. Indoor air gun shooting - the barrel was not rifled, it had a smooth bore - using a small metal dart fitted with a fluffy tail, had a popular following and the clubs in the area competed in a League.

The competitors had to have a steady hold and an accurate aim as the shooting was done in the standing position, at ranges of 6 and 8 yards. Not far you might say, but required concentration on the part of the firer. The block board targets, with defined scoring rings, were illuminated with hooded lamps and the rest of the hall was in darkness.

I found that I could get consistently reasonably high scores. So, during my recruit training in the Royal Marines, I soon discovered that I could fire the heavy service rifle with little difficulty and qualified as a Marksman. The small arms instructor's pet saying was 'Hold, aim and squeeze.'

My service shooting progressed with the encouragement and coaching of the Small Arms Instructors, from service targets to competition targets with more exact scoring areas and smaller Bulls Eyes.

Whilst serving as a Sergeant small arms instructor at the Royal Marines Depot, Deal, Kent during the period 1947/48, I became the Depot Rifle Champion Shot at the annual shooting meeting in 1948, receiving a fine tankard. Basically this was the start of my competition shooting interest.

Over the years I shot on various ranges around the world. There was the Depot range at Kingsdown with chalk cliffs on one side, and on the other the sea of the English Channel, splashing against the firing points. While serving with 42 Commando RM in the Far East we shot on ranges on Stonecutters Island Hong Kong, Ipoh and Port Dixon in Malaya. Then on the other side of the world, when I was a member of a combined Devon/Jersey Team, on ranges at Barbados, Jamaica, Trinidad and British Guiana. 45 Commando RM saw me shooting in the service competitions in Cyprus and Malta, with some training shoots in Tripoli.

Back in the United Kingdom we used ranges at Browndown, Gosport; the Army ranges at Hythe in Kent, and Straight Point, Exmouth, Devon.

The main events of rifle shooting in the UK are held on the National Rifle Association ranges at Bisley, near Woking, Surrey. My first visit to Bisley was in 1947. It was an impressive sight to see Century Range with its 100 targets set along the stop-butts, and the grass covered firing points laid out at distances from the Butts of 200, 300, 400, 500 and 600 yards. Even longer ranges, 900 up to 1200 yards, were nearby just over the hill on Stickledown.

I must say that there is great satisfaction in holding a rifle steady whilst lying on the long range firing point, to pit one's shooting skill against the variations of wind and sunlight and, when the aim is accurate, carefully release the trigger to fire the round, and about two seconds later the bullet hits the thirty inch Bulls Eye 1000 yards away. The full target measured ten feet by six feet. At 200 yards the Bulls Eye was only five inches in diameter, a little smaller than the saucer for an average tea cup, very little room for error.

We used the standard .303 inch calibre British Service Rifle No.4, as issued - Service Rifle Class A (S.R.a.) - for the service events. For the target competitions we used the same make of rifle but fitted with a more sophisticated backsight with vernier scales - this was known as Service Rifle Class B (S.R.b.). The vernier scale enabled us to make very small adjustments for elevation, and to move the eyepiece to the left or right of centre for wind allowances.

During my small arms instructors course we visited a Royal Ordnance factory to see weapons being manufactured, from the foundry to the cutting of the rifling in the barrels in the machine shops. The skill of the workforce came to light at the final inspection and testing stage with the weapons within the very fine tolerances that had to be achieved.

Another visit was to a Royal Arsenal where the .303 inch calibre ammunition was made. Here, also, the manufacture was to very fine limits. The correct weight of the bullet, the right amount of propellant in the brass cartridge case were both fundamental for constant accuracy in shooting. On the rifle range we liked to achieve a grouping capacity of say five rounds within an area of a two inch circle at 100 yards, which all goes to show how important it was to have an excellent rifle and tight grouping ammunition. This detailed knowledge of both weapons and ammunition was of indispensable value to small arms instructors.

We even shot in the rain. There are many stories to be told of shooting in wet weather, 'wet shots' can go anywhere, but usually high over the target. Some competitors just let their rifle and ammunition get wet and made an adjustment to the elevation of the backsight. I much preferred to shoot dry. That is, to keep the breech mechanism of the rifle covered and ammunition dry by the use of towelling and a chamois leather while waiting my turn to shoot.

Spotting the flight or swirl of the bullet through binoculars for a split second as it travels through the air, and watching for the fall of shot as the bullet strikes the ground, are other skills one developed. Equally important are the abilities to coach, watch the wind and call changes in time for the firer to alter his backsight, all very necessary to be successful in team competitions.

The big thrill of the National shooting calendar at Bisley was to get through stages one and two of the Queen's Prize and shoot in the Final Hundred at 900 and 1000 yards on Stickledown.

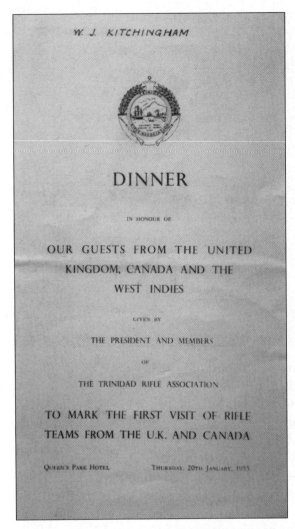

W. J. KITCHINGHAM

DINNER

IN HONOUR OF

OUR GUESTS FROM THE UNITED
KINGDOM, CANADA AND THE
WEST INDIES

GIVEN BY

THE PRESIDENT AND MEMBERS

OF

THE TRINIDAD RIFLE ASSOCIATION

TO MARK THE FIRST VISIT OF RIFLE
TEAMS FROM THE U.K. AND CANADA

QUEEN'S PARK HOTEL   THURSDAY, 20TH JANUARY, 1955

In the eight years from 1954 to 1962 I shot my way through the qualifying stages to the Queen's Final six times. Some 1200 very hopeful competitors from all over the British Commonwealth annually enter stage one of this event. 300 competitors with the highest scores go on to stage two, shooting for a place in the Final Hundred.

In one final I was paired with a competitor from Canada who missed the target ten times. This necessitated the target being carefully checked for a hit each time he fired causing an unacceptable waste of time. The National Rifle Association amended the rules so that when a competitor had a couple of misses he is retired from the shoot.

I was delighted to be selected to shoot for my country, and found myself in the England team, for the first time in 1954, for the National Challenge Trophy. The match is shot at 200, 500 and 600 yards on Century Range between England, Wales, Scotland, and Ireland.

Then 1956 saw me in the England team for the Mackinnon Challenge Cup. This match took place between England, Australia, Canada, Ireland, Wales, Scotland, the British West-Indies, and South Africa at 900 and 1000 yards on the Stickledown Range.

While serving overseas I had a number of successes. I was Brigade Champion Shot in 1951 with 42 Commando RM in Malaya. Then in 1957 with 45 Commando RM I was first in the Individual Rifle event in Cyprus at the District Inter-Services Meeting, and in Malta I was the Inter Service Individual Rifle Champion.

During my shooting career for the Corps, overseas and at Bisley, I shot with some very fine Royal Marine marksmen, men who not only shot for the Corps and England but also made it into the Queen's Final. Amongst the most accomplished were Major S Armour RM, Major H N Cooper RM, Major D L S Langley RM, QMS A Maylor and C/Sgt S E Skippings.

Life-long family friendships developed with Albert Maylor, Wally Mortiboys and

Parade 13·30hrs. No.11 Range.

ENGLAND NATIONAL MATCH TEAM 1954

THURSDAY 14TH JULY 1.45 p.m.

CAPTAIN J.A. BARLOW   ADJUTANT W.J. DRAKE   COACH J.A. BARLOW

Target	1	2	3	4	5
Sub-Coach					
1st Detail	Reynolds. E.G.B. Tribe. G.E.	Hall. J. Kitchingham. W.J.	Wheeler. S.F. Sear H.B.	Laceby-Stevens.C. Baker. E.H.	Bartlett. K.W.W. Hunt. A.C.
2nd Detail	Slocock J.A. Black. D.J.	Turine G.E. Walker. H.F.C.	Kingway. W.H. Blundell R.V.	Fullen. R.A. Seward C.W.	Cantley. D.F. Clarke. F.E.
Reserve.	Westmacott J.B.	Lampton-Fridges. RA	Worth. W. H.	Rommer R.W.	Davies. J. F.F.

The first-named of each pair to be the right hand first. See instructions on leaf.

Peter Willis. There was also Tom Anstey, stalwart and driving force of the Devon Rifle Association. He was always ready to help a young shottist.

Some members of the Royal Marines, unsympathetic to our cause, taunted us as being 'Shottists', 'Gravel Bellies' or 'Pot Hunters', but I was rather struck by the little used nickname 'Smoke-Pole Artists'. I thought it rather good.

Skill-at-arms was recognized many years ago as an important service requirement. The Royal Marines has, therefore, fostered competition shooting through the Royal Marines Rifle Association which was founded in 1896. Over the years, they have maintained a camp at Bisley to house Royal Marines selected to shoot in the Corps Meeting and for the Corps teams in the prestigious Inter-Service and National Rifle Association events.

The short period of a few weeks in June and early July is a busy time for camp staff and competitors. There are many service teams at Bisley, the Royal Navy, the Army, the Royal Air Force, Reserve Units, and overseas teams, all accommodated in their own camps. I used to enjoy the friendly matches against the Canadians, and the Army Small Arms School Corps; and the light hearted swapping of yarns over a glass of beer on a warm summer's evening in our own modest club house the 'Dew Drop Inn'.

I remember when, in 1952, I was a member of the Portsmouth Group RM Team that won the coveted Army Rifle Association Methuen Cup. The Corps next won it in 1992. In my opinion the Methuen Cup winners gold medal is one of the most attractive medals to be won at Bisley in the inter-service events.

In 1953 I shot for the Devon County team at Bisley in the English Twenty Club

County Championships. We won the event and HRH The Duke of Edinburgh arrived on the firing point to present the Devon team with the winners' cup and individual medals.

The author (in foreground) with 45 Commando RM shooting team Inter-Service District Championships 1957 - Dhekelia Cyprus

Photo: "Evening News and Hampshire Telegraph", Portsmouth

'Chairing' the Winner of the Individual Championship Browndown QMS W J KITCHINGHAM RM RM Infantry Training Centre

Albert Maylor, William J Kitchingham, Walter C Mortiboys. Outside the Dewdrop Inn Royal Marines Rifle Association Camp Bisley. July 1984.

Chapter 12
Royal Navy and Royal Marines
careers service

I left Aden in June 1963 and returned to the Infantry Training Centre at Lympstone in Devon. My attention was drawn to The Royal Navy and Royal Marines Careers Service which was calling for volunteers to fill vacancies, as recruiters, at various Careers Offices throughout the United Kingdom. I volunteered and, after a visit to the Department of Naval Recruiting in London for an interview, was informed that I had been accepted and that I would be posted to the Inverness Office on the 15 September 1963.

This entailed selling our home in Exmouth and buying another one in Inverness. I therefore arranged for the local newspaper, The Inverness Courier, to forward copies of their newspaper to enable us to select a likely property from their housing advertisements. One seemed promising so I made a dash to Inverness one Friday, catching the night sleeper train from London, arriving in Inverness on the Saturday morning. The air felt fresh and the sky had a clarity about it.

I had breakfast in a small cafe just inside the market entrance, and afterwards asked a taxi driver to take me to the address, just on the outskirts of town. There I met the family who were selling, and was shown around the house. It was quite new and would suit us just fine. So it was back to town and the solicitor's office where the arrangements were agreed. It was all completed and done with by midday.

I then had a walk around the town and stood for a time by the new road bridge over the River Ness, looking at the flow of the river as it made the short distance to Beauly Firth. That evening, as I caught the night sleeper train to London and then back to Exmouth, I thought this is going to be a good move.

In September, leaving our eldest daughter, Beverley, in Exmouth to continue her education, Patricia and I with our other three young daughters left Devon by car and had a pleasant three day drive to Scotland. We met our furniture removers at our new home as arranged and soon settled in. On the first night it was quite noticeable how much daylight there was at bedtime. We were, of course, 500 miles north of Exmouth.

Next day I reported to Lieutenant Jim Mackintosh BEM (CS) RN, the recruiting officer, and met his assistant, Chief Petty Officer George MacLeod (CS), at the recruiting office. As individuals we took to one another quite well, this was a good start I thought. They were both Scotsmen, Jim from Inverness, and George from Stornoway on the Isle of Lewis.

The office was a rather dull, dowdy, old fashioned place up a flight of stairs in an office block in Union Street. However, a new office was about to be fitted out at a much better location just a few streets away, on the ground floor of a corner property in Academy Street.

Within a few weeks I was sent to London, to join a dozen other new Careers Advisers, for a course on the selection procedures, and other administration matters as required by the Director of Naval Recruiting. The term 'Careers Adviser' had now replaced the old 'Recruiter'. The main aspects of the job were public relations, school liaison and the processing of applicants.

Back in Inverness, and full of enthusiasm, I soon had my first candidate to deal with. All went well and he was accepted for the Royal Navy. Four months later I sent him a travel warrant and joining instructions for the shore based training establishment, HMS Ganges, I wished him well. My mind went back twenty-two years to the time when I first walked through the Main Archway of Stonehouse Barracks Plymouth for my recruit training.

The area from which the Inverness Office drew its candidates was very large, the population being well spread out. It included the counties of Moray, Nairn, Inverness, Ross and Cromarty, Sutherland, Caithness, the Isle of Skye and the Outer Hebrides.

During the summer months, particularly July and August, we would set up recruiting stands at the various County Highand Games venues. Many Highland communities have their own fetes, galas, agricultural shows and games. Some are held in the most scenic locations with the tree covered hills as a backcloth. However, the Nairn Games were held on a grassy area, The Links, the sea overlooking the Moray Firth.

Manning the Careers Stand at these venues gave me the opportunity to watch at close hand the traditional Scottish events. Highland Dancing with the competitors in their dancing costumes and tartan skirts. And the kilted men in the heavyweight competitions such as throwing the weight over the bar, putting the shot, Scots hammer throwing and tossing the caber.

The next few years brought a number of interesting events. I was delighted when I was allocated the two tickets I had applied for when the Royal Marines Corps Tercentenary was celebrated in July 1964. Patricia and I travelled to London on the night sleeper train from Inverness, and attended the Review of the Royal Marines by HM The Queen on the lawns at Buckingham Palace on Thursday 23rd. It was a pleasant day and we had a good view of the parade from seats in the right rear of the stand by the Bow Room steps.

Next day we attended the Service of Thanksgiving at St. Paul's Cathedral held in the presence of the Duke of Edinburgh, Captain General of the Royal Marines. Both events were fully attended by serving and former Royal Marines yet, we met few whom we had known well in Malta or Exmouth. Then it was back to Inverness that night.

At our Careers Office I was quite surprised at how many people called to see Jim

The Massed Pipes and Drums of the 1st Battalion
Queen's Own Highlanders at the Cameron Barracks

or George, and have a chat. There were folk from the Black Isle, the West Coast, the Isle of Skye and Stornoway in fact, from all over the region. I got quite used to it and made a few friends myself. It was nice to see this aspect of life of the people of the Highlands and Islands.

Jim was well known in church circles and helped in the religious services a great deal. George was helpful in raising funds for King George's Fund for Sailors, the Burma Star Association and local youth organisations.

One person who occasionally called was Lieutenant Commander Lachlan R D Mackintosh of Mackintosh RN (Rtd). As Chief of the Clan Mackintosh he held a Clan Gathering and linked it with a Highland Industries Exhibition on the 6 to 8 August 1964 - the last gathering of the Mackintosh Clan had been held in August 1951 by his father.

The 1964 gathering took place at the ancestral home, Moy Hall, just off the main road, the A9, a few miles south-east of Inverness. There were about forty stand holders for the Highland Industries Exhibition, and the three Armed Services were invited to provide recruiting stands.

Jim, George and I were very pleased when The Mackintosh invited our families to the final day. The day when the Clan Mackintosh would be called to gather in front of Moy Hall to receive an address of welcome from The Mackintosh of Mackintosh and then, led by a bagpipe band, march past their Chief. It was a privilege to witness this unique Highland event. There were over one hundred clansfolk from many parts of the world, including from Tulsa City, Oklahoma, Chief Waldo Emerson Chief of the Creek Indian Nation wearing his ceremonial dress. Our five year old daughter, Yvonne, was deeply interested in this and quite puzzled why he was not wearing a tartan like the other people. However, after the Indian Chief briefly explained his family tree to her he invited Yvonne to have her photograph taken with him.

George had warned me shortly after I join the Careers Office in Inverness to be sure to get the spelling of Clan names

A member of the Clan Mackintosh

correct, not least that of Mackintosh. Our headquarters in London kept addressing Jim as MacKintosh (using a capital K) which did not please him.

Inside Moy Hall we had the opportunity to see a few items of history dating back to the 1745 Rising. The Mackintosh pointed out a bonnet worn by Prince Charlie, a four poster bed in which the Prince slept, and many other interesting objects. I was interested in the firearms, swords and history of the period as just over six miles north of May is the battle field of Culloden.

When the nation heard the sad news that Sir Winston Churchill had died on the 24 January 1965, I requested leave, went to London and joined the long queue of people waiting to pay their last respects to a great Englishman, whose body was lying in state in the Great Hall of Westminster. As I shuffled forward in the quiet queue towards the entrance, I reflected on my duties at Quebec, Washington and Yalta, and what a privilege it had been to have served him. It was a sheer coincidence, however, that as I at last filed past the catafalque, it was the turn of four Royal Marine Officers dressed in their blue uniforms who stood in respectful guard on the steps at the corners of the catafalque. I knew one of them quite well; there was a flicker of recognition as our eyes met for a brief moment.

A number of public relations duties came our way as directed by the Regional Careers Staff Officer from his office in Glasgow. On one such occasion I was asked to act as the Inspecting Officer at the 12th Inverness Boys Brigade Company Open Night parade which went very well.

Then there was the time when I acted as one of the judges at the British Legion

Standard Bearer Competition for the Highland and Islands Area. The British Legion does such sterling work for both ex service and serving men and women, I felt it was an honour to take part in their parade.

Another occasion was when Lt Mackintosh received a telephone call from the Regional Careers Staff Officer in Glasgow with instructions to purchase a wreath and to give it to me to lay at the Commando War Memorial at Spean Bridge, near Fort William at the southern end of the Great Glen. It was in the hills, glens and lochs a few miles to the west of Spean Bridge where the Commandos received their wartime training.

I drove along the Loch Ness road from Inverness, past Fort Augustus and on to Spean Bridge, I had calls to make further on at Fort William and Kinlochleven.

After laying the wreath I stepped back, saluted and looked up at the three bronze figures and thought of the lady in London who had her private reason for wanting this tribute to be made. I was pleased to have been of service in this act of remembrance. A lone spray of fresh flowers already lay at the foot of the memorial, it was early June - the Allied Armies landed on the beaches of Normandy on the morning of the 6 June 1944, D-Day, in operation 'Overlord'.

During the early years of World War Two the Commandos were mainly hand-picked volunteers, drawn from almost every regiment in the Army. Then in the Spring of 1942 the first RM Commando unit was formed, and after a period of intensive training was one of the units which took part in the raid on the French coastal town of Dieppe, on the night of 18/19 August 1942.

The Royal Marine Display Team, under the command of Major H N Cooper RM, furnished by 41 Commando RM, came to the Capital of the Highlands in early August 1965 and took part in the Inverness Tattoo. The team's spectacular events certainly impressed the audiences and proved to be an excellent public relations exercise helping us in our recruiting efforts. The spectators went home with the Sunset Ceremony ringing in their ears.

George and I were on recruiting duty in Bught Park on Saturday the 25 June 1966, when the World Pipe Band Championship coupled with a 'Gathering of the Clans' was held in Inverness. Sixty-two Pipe Bands, not only from Scotland but also from overseas countries, competed for the coveted title of top pipe band, which was won by the Muirhead and Sons, Grangemouth Pipe Band. The climax came at the end of the day when the Provost of Inverness took the salute at the march past of the massed bands. With some 1000 pipers and 300 drummers all dressed in their tartan uniforms it was quite a spectical for the eye as well as the ear. Some thirty clans were represented at the 'Gathering', and during the day many people visited the clan tents to look at tartans, crests and badges. I believe many people, especially visitors from overseas, were trying to trace their family tree, to make a connection between their present name and one of the traditional clan names. It was a great event; some 15000 people were estimated to have been present. I was quite worn out when it was time to pack up our recruiting stand and go home.

In 1967 my grandfather, Albert Ardrey, my mother's father, died a few months short of his 101st birthday. He enlisted as a Private with the 2nd Battalion the Royal Scots at Aldershot in 1890, and served in Mandalay until 1898. He came home and went on the Reserve but he was recalled a few months later to the 1st Battalion of the Regiment to fight in the South African War.

When he celebrated his 100th birthday in 1966, the Colonel of the Regiment and the President of the Royal Scots Association visited him at his home in Kent and presented him with a small statuette of a soldier in the regiment's dress of 100 years

Albert Ardrey aged 100 years, 15 October 1966

ago, and a birthday cake made by the Army Catering Corps Training Centre at Aldershot. A Regimental piper in full dress played the bagpipes as a champagne toast was drunk in honour of Albert. It was most thoughtful of the members of the Royal Scots Association to honour an old soldier, and was much appreciated by my mother and family.

Past generations of my family, as was the case with many others in the country, served in the Armed Forces. In World War I, 1914-1918, two of our uncles served in France, one was wounded on the Somme. Then in the years after World War II my two brothers were to serve in the Royal Navy. One became a Chief Shipwright, and the other served his National Service in the Communications Branch.

During our recruiting duties we wore our blue uniforms. A naval officer or a chief petty officer was not out of place, but a Royal Marine Quartermaster Sergeant, dressed in blue uniform with scarlet sash and polished leather belt, in the Scottish Highlands usually drew attention whether it was in Inverness, Thurso or Lochboisdale in South Uist.

The people of the Western Isles, throughout the decades, have provided the Royal Navy with sailors when the call came. Some Island Communities lost most of their adult menfolk when a number from the same locality, serving together in HM ships, were lost in war at sea.

Recruiting duties took me to every major town and just about every village in our region, including the Western Isles, showing Naval recruiting films at schools or

Youth Organizations, and attending Careers Conventions.

We had a sturdy Standard Vanguard car for the purpose and needed it. At the time, the road west to the vehicular ferry at Kyle of Lochalsh for the Isle of Skye was single track in some sections, with pull-in places for vehicles to overtake or pass one another. Some roads even had grass growing between the wheel tracks. I was warned by George to give way to the fish lorries as the drivers made their dash to the fish markets. How right he was! One fish lorry driver forced me off the road onto the soft verge, fortunately I suffered no injury, and there was no damage to the car.

There are some marvellous views from the roads in the North of Scotland and the Western Isles. The narrow road from Kishorn to Applecross in Western Ross, with its tight hairpin bends over the mountain pass was quite an experience. It was said to be one of the highest roads in this part of Scotland.

During my tour of duty in the Highlands I travelled many times up and down both sides of Loch Ness, sometimes stopping by the ruins of Urquhart Castle near Drumnadrochit, or at Foyers on the south east side, to scan the surface of the cold waters of Loch Ness for "Nessie". I was genuinely interested in the phenomenon; both Jim and George told me they had seen the monster. So I put the question, when I had the opportunity, to people living near Loch Ness, even to a teacher at Fort Augustus Abbey School which was built on the south west shore of the Loch "had they ever seen the monster?" At least half a dozen people claimed to have seen the mysterious 'Nessie'.

I once saw a disturbance on the water, a small bow wave, but I dismissed it as being caused by a wind eddy playing on the water. I never saw the Loch Ness Monster - I wonder if a wee dram, or two, of a twelve year old, single Highland Malt whisky would have helped?!

I had been serving at the Inverness Careers Office for five years when I was attracted to a vacancy in the administration section of the Department of Naval Recruiting in London. I volunteered, and was accepted.

I felt a pang of regret, clearly we were going to miss Inverness, miss the friendly atmosphere of the Glen Mhor Hotel where, on those chilly evenings, a cheery log fire burned in the grate of the reception lounge. And from the bay window of its dining room, where we enjoyed some fine evening meals, we would look across the tree lined Ness Bank and watch the river Ness flowing past. The warm sandstone building of St Andrew's Cathedral stood in the background on the far side of the Ness. We would miss those peaceful walks over the footbridges and through the small islands where the river Ness, dividing into a number of branches, flowed past. There were, of course, those keen types who, having paid the necessary fee for their 'beat' stood in their waders, up to their waists in the river casting their fly rods for salmon.

It was now September 1968. We sold our house in Inverness and moved south buying a house on a new estate in Rainham, Kent. The railway station was about ten minutes' walk from home and a regular train service to London, taking about one hour for the journey, was available.

My new job was much in the manner of a Unit Stores Quartermaster Sergeant, looking after the requirements of the forty-eight RN and RM Careers Information Offices located throughout the United Kingdom, all needing a variety of naval stores, from white ensigns for their flag poles to film projectors. There was a steady stream of requests for a fresh supply of recruiting literature and the replacement of worn out recruiting films. A number of excellent models of HM Ships, made by Mr Julian Glossop, were available for use at displays and in Careers Office windows.

The experience of working in a Careers Office was a great advantage to me in my new job; I just got on with it. There was a great feeling of job satisfaction in all sections of the Department of Naval Recruiting which each Director during his tenure of office readily acknowledged.

We had office space in the north wing of the historic Old Admiralty Building in Whitehall. The windows on the south side overlooked Horse Guards Parade where the Queen, on her official birthday, takes the salute at the ceremony of Trooping the Colour.

After a number of years in this building the Department had to move into Archway Block North which, lying close to Trafalgar Square with its fountains and Nelson's column, marked the east end of the Mall.

Although we had the assistance of the staff porters, moving office equipment is an unpleasant and grimy task. However, the new location had been redecorated, but the walls of our new office, which I shared with the section officer, Lieutenant W D Rogers MBE (CS) RN, were painted a hideous yellow colour. There was some consolation however, the window of this small room on the first floor overlooked the Mall which gave us excellent opportunities to witness State processions making their way through Admiralty Arch and along the Mall to Buckingham Palace.

Over the years and in many places around the world, including Horse Guards Parade, the Royal Marines have taken part in many ceremonial parades, Drum-head Services, Tattoos and 'Beating Retreat'.

To my mind the Royal Marines Corps of Drums and massed bands 'Beating Retreat' has always been an emotional spectacle, tugging at one's 'heart-strings'. I have often noticed a moist eye and a tear trickle down the cheeks of old soldiers watching the event.

Although listening to the musicians playing the Evening Hymn, and the buglers with their clear ringing notes on the Corps silver bugles sounding 'Sunset', I felt sure they, as with me, were really reflecting on the memories of their service years and of the close friends they once knew.

Owing to the long service of Careers Advisers, vacancies in Careers Offices were determinable years ahead, so I placed my name on the list for the Chatham Careers Office. In May 1975 I left the Department of Naval Recruiting in London for Chatham and there joined the staff, one of whom I knew very well having served with him, Quartermaster Sergeant A E Smith RM, a drill instructor. The office was twenty minutes' drive by car from home, some difference from the daily rail journey to Whitehall and return, of which I had grown weary.

I was due to leave the Royal Marines on pension in April 1979, so it was time to plan my future employment in a civilian capacity. I did not wish to be in a job which required travelling to London; I had had enough of that, travelling daily by rail for nearly seven years. A job within a radius of twenty miles from Rainham was my hope.

In between my recruiting duties I began to take an interest in the Services Resettlement Bulletins which were published periodically. My application for resettlement briefing was approved by the Director of Naval Recruiting, and my name forwarded to the Department of Naval Education Services which arranged resettlement courses for Royal Naval & Royal Marine personnel leaving the service.

My preparation for a Second Career commenced with two sessions at the South West London College. The first was on Self Analysis, a prerequisite to the production of a Curriculum Vitae (CV), and proved of immense value to me. The second session was on The Interview. As Careers Advisers we were well trained in interviewing and question technique. So, to become the interviewee instead of the interviewer was, I suppose, a psychological hurdle to cross.

There is camaraderie in the service and a feeling of belonging to a group of people which is severed on going to pension. I knew of three Careers Advisers who found the shock of adjusting to civilian life most difficult.

Next came a counselling session with a civilian employment officer. As Safety Law was assuming greater importance with the introduction of the Health and Safety at work Act, I was advised to consider taking a course to qualify as an Industrial Safety Officer. This seemed like good advice to me; I felt easy with the idea.

In January 1978 I was one of eighty-seven officers and SNCOs who attended a two-day Careers Briefing at the Plymouth College of Further Education, to give us an insight into the job of an Industrial Safety Officer.

By lunch time on the first day and at the invitation of the course co-ordinator those who felt the job was not for them had permission to return to their units. At the end of the second day there were only thirty of us remaining who wanted to continue.

A few weeks later I was very pleased to be allocated a place on a course which would run from 6 November 1978 to the 15 December 1978. I was now looking forward to a Second Career.

When the time came, accommodation was provided for me in the Sergeants' Mess, Stonehouse Barracks.

The Plymouth College of Further Education was a comfortable walking distance from the Barracks, and this gave me much needed exercise in the mornings and evenings. It was a full time course, requiring a lot of sitting in the lecture rooms, thirty-nine hours a week for six weeks.

At fifty-four years of age I was nicknamed the geriatric of the class. Well, I sat the examinations and obtained a useful qualification for a job in the 'outside world'.

I am grateful to the Services Resettlement Officers for their good advice, and to the Course Tutors of the Plymouth College of Further Education for preparing me so well for the examinations.

Following my discharge from the Royal Marines, I spent ten interesting years in Local Government as a Health and Safety Officer.

Somehow it seemed fitting that I should have been accommodated in Stonehouse Barracks during my preparation for a second career. After all, it was here thirty-seven years ago that I walked through the archway of the main gate to commence my recruit training.

Yvonne Small and Margaret Stott, two of Bill Kitchingham's daughters, presenting his medals to the Royal Marines Museum at the RMHS' 50th Anniversary Dinner 24 October 2014

THE MERITORIOUS SERVICE MEDAL

is awarded to

Warrant Officer 2 W.J. Kitchingham

S004130G

in recognition of

long, dedicated and meritorious service

in the Royal Marines

Gordon Tait

Admiral
Second Sea Lord

30th March, 1979

MSM certificate